THE LEAGUE

THE LEAGUE

THE LEAGUE

THE TRUE STORY OF AVERAGE AMERICANS ON THE HUNT FOR WWI SPIES

Bill Mills

Skyhorse Publishing

Skyhorse Publishing books may be purchased in bulk at special discounts for sales promotion, corporate gifts, fund-raising, or educational purposes. Special editions can also be created to specifications. For details, contact the Special Sales Department, Skyhorse Publishing, 307 West 36th Street, 11th Floor, New York, NY 10018 or info@skyhorsepublishing.com.

Skyhorse® and Skyhorse Publishing® are registered trademarks of Skyhorse Publishing, Inc.®, a Delaware corporation.

www.skyhorsepublishing.com

10 9 8 7 6 5 4 3 2 1

Library of Congress Cataloging-in-Publication Data

Mills, Bill, 1958-
  The League : the true story of average Americans on the hunt for WWI spies / Bill Mills.
    p. cm.
  ISBN 978-1-62087-508-7 (hbk. : alk. paper) 1. American Protective League. 2. World War, 1914-1918–Secret service–United States. 3. Espionage, German–United States–History–20th century. 4. Sabotage–United States–History–20th century. 5. Spies–United States–History–20th century. 6. Draft resisters–United States. 7. Industrial Workers of the World. 8. World War, 1914-1918–United States. I. Title. II. Title: True story of average Americans on the hunt for WWI spies.
  D619.3.M55 2013
  940.3'73–dc23

                                    2013004364

Printed in the United States of America

For my parents

CONTENTS

ACKNOWLEDGMENTS

The idea for this book came about while I was reading a history of the American home front during World War I. Finding a brief reference to the American Protective League, I was amazed to learn that a private organization of civilian volunteers had been formed during the war to investigate cases for the Justice Department. In attempting to learn more, I discovered that very little had been published about the League, and the information that was available appeared incomplete or of questionable veracity. I decided to write a book of my own that would give a complete and balanced account.

My interest in the League remained undiminished throughout the course of this project. Whether it has been the thrill of revealing a long-forgotten secret world, or the chance to experience the America that my grandparents lived in and contrast how an earlier generation dealt with domestic security in time of crisis, the saga of the American Protective League has proven to be a fascinating tale. I hope that you enjoy reading *The League* as much as I enjoyed writing it.

As can be imagined, locating information about a secret organization that existed nearly 100 years ago was a challenge. Fortunately, a number of institutions and individuals were there to provide assistance to me. The Department of Special Collections of the University of California at Los Angeles is the

ACKNOWLEDGMENTS

repository of the Charles Daniel Frey Papers, the finest collection of original documents related to the American Protective League in existence, and its staff was extremely helpful in making the collection available to me. The Department of Rare Books, Special Collections and Preservation at the University of Rochester houses a fine collection of New York American Protective League documents, including *The Hidden Menace,* the unfinished, unpublished history of the New York APL Division written in 1919. Manuscript Librarian Lori Birrell was very helpful during my research there. Teresa Sromek of the Newberry Library in Chicago kindly assisted me by providing information on Operative Bernard Lichtenstadt's family history. Finally, special thanks to Leila Lott and Kay Edwards for relating the story of how B.L. Lichtenstadt's APL documents were unearthed in Tennessee.

Bill Mills
Concord, Massachusetts

Spies and Lies

German agents are everywhere, eager to gather scraps of news about our men, our ships, our munitions. It is still possible to get such information through to Germany, where thousands of these fragments—often individually harmless—are patiently pieced together into a whole which spells death to American soldiers and danger to American homes.

But while the enemy is most industrious in trying to collect information, and his systems élaborate, he is *not* superhuman—indeed he is very often stupid, and would fail to get what he wants were it not deliberately handed to him by the carelessness of loyal Americans.

Do not discuss in public, or with strangers, any news of troop and transport movements, of bits of gossip as to our military preparations, which come into your possession.

Do not permit your friends in service to tell you—or write you—"inside" facts about where they are, what they are doing and seeing.

Do not become a tool of the Hun by passing on the malicious, disheartening rumors which he so eagerly sows. Remember he asks no better service than to have you spread his lies of disasters to our soldiers and sailors, gross scandals in the Red Cross, cruelties, neglect and wholesale executions in our camps, drunkenness and vice in the Expeditionary Force, and other tales certain to disturb American patriots and to bring anxiety and grief to American parents.

And do not wait until you catch someone putting a bomb under a factory. Report the man who spreads pessimistic stories, divulges—or seeks—confidential military information, cries for peace, or belittles our efforts to win the war.

Send the names of such persons, even if they are in uniform, to the Department of Justice, Washington. Give all the details you can, with names of witnesses if possible—show the Hun that we can beat him at his own game of collecting scattered information and putting it to work. The fact that you made the report will not become public.

You are in contact with the enemy *today* just as truly as if you faced him across No Man's Land. In your hands are two powerful weapons with which to meet him—discretion and vigilance. *Use them.*

COMMITTEE ON PUBLIC INFORMATION

8 JACKSON PLACE, WASHINGTON, D. C.

George Creel, Chairman
The Secretary of State
The Secretary of War
The Secretary of the Navy

Contributed through the Div. of Advertising

U. S. Gov't Comm. on Public Information

This space contributed for the Winning of the War by
THE PUBLISHER OF REVIEW OF REVIEWS

"Spies and Lies" was a magazine and poster advertising campaign run in the Fall of 1917 by the Committee on Public Information, an agency created by Executive Order of Woodrow Wilson to influence public opinion in support of the war.

PROLOGUE

CHICAGO, WEST SIDE, FEBRUARY 1918. The late afternoon sun had nearly disappeared from the sky, replaced by the ghostly twilight now beginning to descend over the city. A passing snow shower that had started a few minutes before gave the streets and sidewalks a white crystalline glow beneath the darkening sky. It had been another bone-chilling winter day in Chicago and was becoming even colder, due to a blustery current of Canadian air blowing in off Lake Michigan.

The man standing in the archway of a worn brownstone near Haymarket Square didn't seem to mind. He pulled the brim of his black Homburg lower on his forehead and raised the collar of his heavy black overcoat to protect the back of his neck from the falling snow. His attention wasn't on the weather. It was on a man seated in a warm office, in the bakery across the street.

He had been observing the baker for days, ever since a report had come in that he'd been overheard speaking German to one of his customers. It had been a small courtesy to an elderly patron, but since then, every aspect of the baker's life had come under scrutiny. An operative at the baker's bank had reviewed all of his past personal and business transactions. A complete record of his telephone and telegraph use had been obtained from the Chicago Telephone Company by the Bureau of Investigation for examination by other operatives. Under a variety of pretexts, his neighbors and various business acquaintances had all been interviewed. An operative in the flour trade had contacted the mill that supplied flour to the bakery in order to ascertain whether it was acting in accordance with the local Food Administrator's guidelines. The baker's home had also been surreptitiously entered and searched in minute detail.

The facts were undeniable. The baker was an unregistered enemy alien. Documents found in the warrantless search of his home proved that before emigrating to the United States he had been a member of a Prussian Guard Reserve Regiment, making him a potential future saboteur. Additionally, the baker's past flour purchases from his flour mill greatly exceeded purchases of other cereals, a violation of US Government Food Administration rationing guidelines.

Within twenty-four hours the baker would be arrested under an order of internment.

The man in the black overcoat continued to brave the cold while waiting for the baker to exit his shop. He wished the man would hurry. He himself was a full-time traveling salesman, with a rush order that he needed to deliver to the company office before quitting time. Shadowing the baker to his home, where other operatives would continue surveillance into the night, was his last assignment for the day.

A passing patrolman soon spotted him standing in the archway. The policeman crossed the street and resolutely marched up the steps to challenge him. Before the officer could speak, the man in the black overcoat flashed his leather card case and said "American Protective League." The policeman took a look at his commission card and, with a friendly nod, continued his foot patrol down the sidewalk.

Across the street, the baker at last exited his darkened shop and began to make his way home. The man in the black overcoat shadowed him a safe distance behind. One after another, the pair disappeared into the swirling haze of a passing snow shower . . .

KNOXVILLE, JULY 2008. It was going to be a hot day in eastern Tennessee and Leila Lott wasn't looking forward to it. Leila ran Estate Solutions, a company that specialized in settling estates for inheritors by appraising the contents of a home and then conducting a sale of the previous owner's belongings. It was hard work. With each contract, a houseful of items had to be cleaned, sorted, priced, and readied for sale. The pre-sale cataloging alone would mean many hours spent searching through musty closets, the inevitably dank humid basement, and a hot dusty attic—hopefully without discovering rodents or other unpleasant surprises.

Today's project was the Marx estate, an older house located in one of the better neighborhoods in Knoxville. In the ten years that she'd been in the business Leila had conducted scores of estate sales. Old homes were typically modernized over time, gradually updated with new furniture and furnishings. But the Marx residence was an exception. It had been owned by the Marx family since the 1930s and remained frozen in the style of that era: vintage lace curtains, solid mahogany furniture, and colorful Sarouk oriental carpeting. It seemed more like a museum than a home.

Leila had visited the place a month before to do the appraisal and had gone through most of the house once already—everything except the attic. At the time of her last visit, the heirs' administrator couldn't decide whether to hire Leila for the appraisal alone, or to both appraise and sell the contents of the house, and she didn't want to pay Leila's hourly appraisal fee to "look over the rubbish in the attic." She later changed her mind.

Using a key that the administrator had provided, Leila entered the house with her assistant, Kay Edwards, and prepared to explore the attic. On a second floor landing surrounded by floral wallpaper, the pair donned dust masks and work gloves, switched on powerful flashlights, then lowered the rickety attic climbing ladder and ascended into the black opening in the ceiling. It was like stepping through the door of a blast furnace; the temperature in the unventilated attic was well over 100 degrees Fahrenheit.

Hunched low in the confined space and sweating profusely, the two women surveyed their surroundings. The compact, angled attic was layered in dust and had apparently lain undisturbed for a generation. At some point, planking had been nailed to the crossbeams along the center, creating a makeshift floor. Kay's flashlight beam cut through the darkness, revealing an open steamer trunk filled with antiquated clothing and a few folded horse blankets. Leila could see boxes of old photographs, the most prominent a large sepia-toned portrait of a pretty ballerina, her broad smile frozen in time. Nearby sat a pile of Christmas gifts, still in their wrapping.

"We're going to have to move all this stuff downstairs to appraise it," sighed Leila, and the pair began the tiresome job of walking each item down the ladder to the landing below. Soon the hallway was overflowing with an eclectic assortment of dusty artifacts.

As the remnants in the attic dwindled, Kay noticed a metal box wedged into a corner. On her hands and knees she shimmied close enough to grab it, then carried it downstairs into the daylight. The box was made of black-color stamped steel and looked very old. With the excitement of an archaeologist unearthing an ancient relic, Leila raised the lid and reached inside—only to withdraw a handful of old bills and accounting statements. Anxiously she poured out the remaining contents, and an assortment of aged paper items tumbled in a pile onto the hall rug.

The most striking object was a large framed document. It was yellowed and looked like an old diploma. She peered closely and read:

American Protective League - Chicago Division. Know All Men By These Presents That Operative B.L. Lichtenstadt has loyally and faithfully served the American Protective League in the execution of the various duties assigned to it by the Government of the United States in the prosecution and winning of the World War and in token of appreciation of a work well done is entitled to this Honorable Discharge.

Moving the framed certificate aside, Leila saw a small black and white photograph of a gaunt, unsmiling man with deep bags under his eyes. Kay reached down and picked up a piece of faded newsprint and carefully unfolded the brittle paper. It was an old newspaper article about the same man that included a later photo in which his hair had grayed slightly and he was now wearing steel-rimmed glasses. The caption under the photo read "Mr. B. L. Lytton." She returned it to the pile on the floor and picked up a small blue card, similar to a library card, that was stamped "Sept. 1918" in red ink on both sides. Peering closer, they read: "POLICE DEPARTMENT, CITY OF CHICAGO, Reporter's Pass." The card gave "Mr. William McCormick, employed by the Evening American, the right to pass through Chicago Police Lines wherever formed to obtain news for the press." It too was placed back on the pile.

Scanning across the collection of artifacts, Leila spied a tattered black leather billfold. Inside was a membership card of some sort. It was titled "American Protective League, Organized with Approval and Operating Under the Direction of the United States Department of Justice, Bureau of Investigation." The card had been issued to Operative B. L. Lichtenstadt, Chicago Division. She quickly rifled through the remaining items. There was a small gray pamphlet that was unmarked on the outside except for "Book No. 125, C.N. 7292" and a few pieces of correspondence in envelopes with 1917 and 1918 postmarks addressed to B. L. Lichtenstadt. The envelopes had no sender's name in the upper left corner, only the stamp "Room 1103, 130 N. Wells Street, Chicago Illinois."

Leila returned the items to the metal box.

What was the "American Protective League," she wondered? And who was B. L. Lichtenstadt? Although she had no idea at the time, Leila had opened a window into a long-forgotten chapter of history; the largest organization of secret agents ever to operate on American soil. It was a chapter that began ninety-one years before in the mind of one man: A. M. Briggs of Chicago.

CHAPTER 1

"IT TAKES A SPY TO CATCH A SPY"

Albert Martin Briggs was the kind of man you *had* to like, and in his profession as an advertising sales executive, that was a valuable asset to have. Advertising is an "intangible" product and selling it to a customer requires the very best that a salesman has to offer. Aside from a winning personality, you also have to be smart—able to quickly analyze a customer's needs and develop the right advertising program to deliver results, and you have to be persuasive and present well—be able to "make the pitch", in a way that will convince a customer to hire your firm over the potential competitors waiting in the wings.

Briggs had been eminently successful at his trade. He was a pioneer in the field of outdoor billboard advertising, which he had entered in the mid-1890s with the Gunning System, a major outdoor advertising syndicate of the day. Eight years later Briggs formed the outdoor advertising department of the J. Walter Thompson advertising agency with headquarters in Chicago, even today one of the largest and most prestigious advertising agencies in the country. In 1911 he formed the A. M. Briggs Company in Cleveland, later moving his headquarters to

Chicago. In 1916 Briggs merged his firm with a group of other companies to form the Poster Advertising Company, taking a position as Vice President in the new organization.

A. M. Briggs personally developed and handled the Ligget & Myers Tobacco Company account, as well as Aunt Jemima flour, Gold Dust Powder, Fisk Tires, and two of the leading automobile manufacturers: Saxon Motor Car and Chalmers Motor Companies. Under his direction, employees of his company had developed and managed the outdoor advertising for the Wrigley Gum, Pillsbury Flour, Standard Oil of Indiana, Jello, American Express, Post Toasties, and Collier's Magazine accounts.

His expanding advertising business brought him great wealth. At the time of his death Briggs owned a home in Garden City, Long Island, worth $4 to $5 million in today's values. There he lived with his wife Anna and their daughter Priscilla— and five servants. He also maintained a summer home on Bemus Point, and was well known by the residents of the Chautauqua Lakes region, where it was said that he owned the finest boat on the lake.

In addition to money, Briggs's business dealings had brought him a degree of power and influence. He regularly dealt with the senior management and principals of some of the largest companies in the nation. This in turn gave him entry into the leading clubs and associations. He belonged to the Cherry Valley Club golf course, The Question, and several country clubs and was a member of the Board of Governors of the Lambs, a trustee of the St. Giles Hospital for Crippled Children, and an organizer of the Advertising Association of the World.

Briggs was the quintessential self-made man of the late-nineteenth century. Born on January 12, 1874, to a middle-class family in Buffalo, New York, he was a graduate of the New York public school system. Like many of the era, Briggs was a strong believer in civic responsibility and public service. In his advertising role, he was chairman of a committee that placed "religious and uplift" posters throughout the United States and Canada to promote church attendance. In 1893, at the age of nineteen (young even for that period), Briggs was appointed a second lieutenant in the 65ᵗʰ Regiment of the New York State National Guard. Five years later he was a volunteer in the Spanish-American War and saw service in Cuba.

This was the man that in late-February 1917 visited the office of the US Justice Department in Chicago to call on Hinton G. Clabaugh, division superintendent of the Bureau of Investigation, to offer an extraordinary proposition. Briggs had met Clabaugh some time before, in regard to a Justice Department investigation, and was well aware that the Bureau of Investigation was in desperate straits.

World War I had begun three years before, triggered by the assassination of an Austrian archduke by a Serbian-connected Bosnian nationalist. The countries of Europe were divided into two camps by a series of pre-war alliances and quickly marched off to war. On one side were the Central Powers of Germany, Austria-Hungary, Bulgaria, and the Ottoman Empire, and on the other, the Allied Powers of France, England, Italy, and Russia. After the failure of the initial German offensive to achieve a knock-out blow, the opposing armies engaged in a series of tactical maneuvers, each attempting to outflank the other, while moving steadily northward until they soon faced each other across thousands of miles of layered trench works and barbed wire that extended from Switzerland to the North Sea. Neither side was able to break through their opponent's defensive positions, and the world soon witnessed battles fought on a scale never seen before, resulting in enormous casualties, after which the battle lines scarcely changed at all. During the battle of Verdun, the French and German armies each experienced 350,000 casualties. In the battle of the Somme, the Allied forces (primarily Britain) suffered 630,000 casualties, while the German army lost 660,000 casualties. On the *first day* of the battle of the Somme 20,000 British soldiers were killed. By the year 1917, neither side held any strategic or tactical advantage, and the conflict remained mired in bloody stalemate.

From the outset of the war America had proclaimed itself neutral. But this neutrality meant that American companies could still supply arms and equipment to either side. With an English blockade in place to prevent supplies from reaching the Central Powers, this meant that in reality American shipments could only reach the Allied forces. Through agents in the United States, Germany (and, later, Austria-Hungary) did whatever they could to disrupt the flow of supplies to England, France, and Russia—short of any action that could be traced back to them and result in the United States joining the war. Between 1914 and 1917 America became a neutral battleground for the warring powers, with both sides engaged in relentless propaganda campaigns attempting to win American public opinion to their side.

The US Justice Department's Bureau of Investigation (renamed the *Federal* Bureau of Investigation in 1935) was one of the principal government agencies tasked with monitoring the activities of these foreign agents and preventing violations of neutrality from taking place on US shores. But the Bureau of Investigation was woefully short on resources and manpower. Within the total US population of 98 million people in 1917, there were 8 million German-Americans and 4.5 million Irish-Americans (many hostile to England after the Easter Rebellion of 1916). There were also 2 million German and Austro-Hungarian aliens residing in the United States, including an estimated 500,000 German army and navy reservists. To counter this mass of potential enemy agents, spies, and saboteurs, the Bureau of Investigation fielded a force of less than 400 special agents, supported by an equally meager annual budget appropriation. Congress had been reluctant to expand the bureau, which would have created an increasingly costly federal bureaucracy to support.

Albert Briggs's timing could not have been better for the proposition that he had in mind. With Germany's resumption of unrestricted submarine warfare the United States broke off diplomatic relations with Germany on February 1, 1917, and war was clearly imminent. Arriving punctually at Clabaugh's office in the Federal Building in Chicago, the stocky, forty-four-year-old ad man was immediately ushered inside to meet the superintendent.

Briggs came directly to the point. "Diplomatic relations with Germany have been severed, and in all probability this country will be drawn into the European War. I volunteered for the war with Spain twenty years ago, and although I'm now physically unable to join the fighting forces, I would like to help in some way. It occurred to me that a volunteer organization might be of great assistance to an investigating bureau such as the one with which you are connected. I will pledge all of my time and resources to such an organization, and I earnestly hope that if you can think of any way in which I can be of assistance to this bureau that you will command me."

Brigg's offer took Superintendent Clabaugh by surprise, particularly since the vice president of the Poster Advertising Company had no experience of any kind in investigatory work. But he was clearly intelligent and sincere in his desire to provide assistance. He was also a man of influence in the business community. Clabaugh thanked Briggs for his offer and told him that he would need some time to consider it.

A few days later, Briggs's phone rang. "Look, I could get ten times as much done if I had the men and money to work with," Clabaugh said. "There are thousands of men who are enemies of this country and ought to be behind bars, but it takes a spy to catch a spy, and I've got a dozen spies to catch a hundred thousand spies right here in Chicago. They have motor cars against my men who have to take street cars. They're supplied with all the money they want; my own funds are limited. We're not at war. All this is civil work. We simply haven't the ways and means to meet the emergency . . ."

"I've been thinking about your idea," Clabaugh continued, "and I believe that an organization of volunteers would be of very great help to our department. As a first step in connection with such an organization, we could use some automobiles which would enable our special agents to cover several times as much territory, to say nothing of the time thus saved, but there is no appropriation from which the government could pay for the upkeep of such cars." Clabaugh was testing the waters before offering support for Briggs's volunteer group. As a first step, could the businessman find a way to satisfy the bureau's immediate need for motor transport?

Briggs rose to the challenge.

"I can get ten or twenty good, quiet men with cars who'll work for nothing," he responded. "They'll take either their business time or their leisure time, or both, and join forces with you. I know we're not at war, but we're all Americans together."

A short time later, Briggs went further. He informed Clabaugh that he was ready to provide, free of charge, four cars for the use of the Bureau of Investigation in Chicago, four automobiles for the bureau in New York, and three more for the use of the Washington bureau office. Briggs also offered a gift of an additional fifty to seventy-five automobiles that he had persuaded a group of Chicago businessmen to donate. These could be divided up among various Bureau of Investigation offices in all of the principal US cities where they could be employed to the best advantage—all at no cost to the government whatsoever.

Clabaugh sent an immediate telegram to his superior in Washington, A. Bruce Bielaski, chief of the Bureau of Investigation, informing him of Briggs's offer and requesting approval to proceed. After assuring Bielaski that acceptance of the offer of automobiles would "not be used as an advertisement in any way" by adman Briggs, Bielaski signaled his approval.

Armed with a letter of introduction provided by the Chicago superintendent, Briggs traveled to Washington to meet in person with Bielaski and other senior Justice Department officials including Wesley Brown, the special assistant to the attorney general, and the private secretary to the attorney general, John Suter. During these meetings, Briggs reiterated his desire to provide support for the Bureau of Investigation by means of a civilian volunteer organization, and he learned firsthand about the obstacles that the Department faced in confronting potential enemies in the United States. The same investigative techniques used to collect advertising data, he likely suggested, could also be used to good effect in gathering intelligence on potentially hostile groups and individuals.

Bielaski was impressed by the Chicago advertising executive. Here was a man who could understand the bureau's problems and martial the resources necessary to provide a solution. Briggs wasn't just a smooth-talking businessman; the large quantity of automobiles that he had obtained for the Bureau proved that.

Returning to Chicago in mid-March 1917 with the knowledge and guidance he had gleaned from meeting with the Justice Department officials in Washington, Briggs set down on paper an outline for his proposed volunteer organization. He delivered the plan in a letter to Clabaugh, who then forwarded it to Bielaski:

Hinton G. Clabaugh
Bureau of Investigation, Chicago

My Dear Mr. Clabaugh:

Believing that the Department of Justice is at this time in need of possible assistance in their work and that a volunteer organization, properly built and controlled, could render valuable and efficient service, I beg to submit the following for your consideration:

Its Purpose: A volunteer organization to aide the Bureau of Investigation of the Department of Justice.

The Object: To work with and under the direction of the Chief of the Bureau of Investigation, of the Department of Justice, or such attorney, or persons as he may direct, rendering such service as may be required from time to time.

Membership: This organization is to be composed of citizens of good moral character who shall volunteer their services and who are acceptable to your Department.

Construction: It is proposed that national headquarters be established either in Washington, or perhaps Chicago, because of its geographical location, and that branch organizations be established in such cities as your Department may direct.

Finances: It is proposed that headquarters organization and branch organizations shall finance themselves either by outside subscriptions or by its members.

Control: It is proposed that each unit of this organization shall be under the control of the Government but will report to and be under the direction of the nearest Department of Justice headquarters.

Trusting you will give the foregoing your consideration.

(Signed) A. M. Briggs

After reviewing the draft organizational charter, Chief Bielaski notified Clabaugh that he should encourage Briggs in the organization of a volunteer association that would aid the Bureau in securing information on the activities of foreign governments and unfriendly aliens. The organization "should be handled as confidentially as practicable and care taken that nothing is done by it to unnecessarily alarm aliens in the US or cause them any apprehension as to the manner with which they will be treated."

Briggs met with Bielaski again on March 22, 1917, to discuss plans for the new volunteer organization. Relations between the United States and Germany had deteriorated in the three weeks since Briggs's first meeting with Clabaugh. Already newspapers were detailing the sweeping measures that the government would put into effect after the declaration of war that was expected when Congress reconvened on the second of April. One of the principal cabinet decisions being reported was that "every department of the government would rush preparedness measures to consummation" and that the (impending) war would be vigorously prosecuted. Against this backdrop, the results of Briggs's second meeting with Bielaski were, in the advertising man's words, "very satisfactory." The chief of the Bureau of Investigation approved Briggs's plan for a volunteer force and requested that it be formed immediately.

Albert Briggs, a successful business executive with no investigative, law enforcement, counter-espionage, or government administrative experience, had just been given authority by the Justice Department to organize a nationwide intelligence-gathering operation. Whether it was the threat of an impending national crisis, the lack of any apparent alternative for the under-staffed federal agency, or the advertising executive's extensive business contacts and his ability to "sell the project," Albert M. Briggs would now lead a secret organization that within a year would grow to over 250,000 members from every social and economic class, employed in virtually every occupation, significant company, and industry in the United States.

It would become the largest secret service in history.

CHAPTER 2

ORGANIZING THE AMERICAN PROTECTIVE LEAGUE

After receiving government approval to proceed, Briggs left Washington aboard a fast express train bound for Chicago to face the daunting task of building a nationwide intelligence organization from scratch. Within days, the United States would be at war with Germany, and Briggs, characteristically a man of high energy and enthusiasm, was anxious to get started. He realized that he'd need the assistance of someone with experience in large-scale clandestine operations to succeed in the effort, and the well-connected advertising executive knew just the man to help: Captain T. B. Crockett.

Briggs had served in the Spanish-American War in Cuba as a lieutenant in the 65th Regiment of the New York State National Guard. A few years later, Thomas B. Crockett, related to the Davy Crocket of Alamo fame, had served as a lieutenant in the 36th US Volunteer Infantry during the Philippine Insurrection. Lasting from 1899 to 1902, the conflict in the Philippines was a vicious guerilla war waged by insurgent bands in armed struggle against the US military. From the mountains of Northwestern Luzon to the low-lying provinces of Morong and Infanta, native Philippine forces, under a handful of leaders, resisted the United States through a campaign of terror and assassination. They were bolstered by a secret society called the Katipunan, whose goal was the death of all Americans and any Philippine villagers and their families friendly to them. It was a war of guile and deception. A major turning point in the struggle occurred when the driving force behind the insurgency, the rebel leader Emilio Aguinaldo, was captured. This came about on the morning of March 24, 1901, when a weary contingent of eighty-four Philippine soldiers tramped into Aguinaldo's encampment to present him with a trophy: five captured American soldiers. But it was a trick: the soldiers dressed in Philippine Army uniforms and carrying Philippine weapons were actually disguised Macabebe troops loyal to the Americans and under the command of their supposed "prisoners"—US Army General Frederick Funston and four of his officers. The US-led force quickly overpowered the rebel troops and seized Aguinaldo. Shipped off to Manila, Aguinaldo was compelled to swear an oath of allegiance to the US government and issue a proclamation to his followers to lay down their weapons and abandon the struggle.

The American troops in the Philippines were secretly aided by a network of paid spies recruited from the indigenous population. In a day without "black" budget allocations for intelligence expenditures, the Army's public appropriation in 1901 included $2.4 million authorized for incidental expenses, among which were the "hire of laborers in the Quartermaster's Department including the hire of interpreters, spies, and guides for the army." The Philippine secret service that was created with these funds proved to be worth every penny spent, providing valuable intelligence to the men battling the insurgents.

Posted to the mountainous region of Northern Luzon, Lieutenant Crockett excelled at this shadow warfare. In February 1901, Crockett led a force of Ilocano scouts north of Bosoboso, where they captured a Philippine prisoner after a skirmish with some of the rebel leader Geronimo's men. Based on information from the prisoner, Crockett then led his men on an all-night march in order to catch a distant rebel outpost unawares at daybreak. In the ensuing eight months, Crockett commanded Ilocano scouts from the sixth district on a number of successful missions: seizing hidden food and weapons storehouses, attacking insurgents at Dummirri and Novaliches, and capturing several guerillas of rebel leader Angele's band in Abra. During these patrols he recruited agents for the Philippine secret service and was the beneficiary of the information that they provided. The high point of Crockett's service in the Philippines came in April 1901, when he led a company of native scouts into Abra and captured a Philippine army major, a lieutenant, and four rebel soldiers. When Lieutenant Thomas B. Crockett returned to the United States the following year he was promptly promoted to Captain.

Fifteen years later another war loomed, and from offices in the Peoples Gas Company building in Chicago, provided "free of charge" to the nascent organization by Samuel Insull of Commonwealth Edison, the two Army veterans, Albert Briggs (who had been a lieutenant in the 65th Regiment of the New York State National Guard during the Spanish-American War in Cuba), general superintendent of the newly named "American Protective League," and T. B. Crockett, his assistant general superintendent, began soliciting business leaders to man the home-front army.

During the first weeks, efforts were concentrated on cities with a large population of German aliens and German immigrants: Chicago, New York, Milwaukee, St. Louis, and Philadelphia. A rudimentary organizational structure was established with a "chief" in charge of each local organization directing subordinate captains, lieutenants, and members. From the nondescript APL headquarters, a stream of letters and telegrams were dispatched to Briggs's wide circle of business contacts and acquaintances, as well as to local chambers of commerce and boards of trade. Men unable to accept a position as chief within their locale were asked to recommend another man of equal caliber within the community. Long-distance phone calls and personal visits were made by Briggs to "the live-wires of the business world"; successful men in their field or city, "big men, brave and able" who could organize and lead a League detachment.

"Mr. Briggs is a gentleman whose personality, persuasive tongue, and nimble mind have suffered no diminishment by reason of success in commerce," a League member wrote of this formative period. "It would have been difficult indeed to have selected another man so admirably fitted for the work he was now to undertake. For months Mr. Briggs travelled throughout the country. He visited state after state, and city after city, and in every section he met with instant response. The idea 'took' as no idea like it had ever taken before. It wasn't necessary to 'sell' anyone—as soon as anyone heard the idea he 'sold' himself."

General Superintendent Briggs's proposition to these men was a direct and persuasive call to duty:

> I have been authorized by the United States Department of Justice, Bureau of Investigation to organize confidentially in your town, a division of the American Protective League. You have been recommended to me as a man possessing the necessary qualifications to successfully organize and command the organization, and I will be glad to have you accept the responsibility of building the organization in your town and acting as its Chief. The object of the American Protective League, which is entirely a patriotic one, no member of which accepts any compensation whatever for his services, is to work under the direction of the United States Department of Justice, Bureau of Investigation, in assisting the Department in securing information on the activities of agents of foreign governments, or persons unfriendly to this government for the protection of private property, etc. Your organization should be made up of American citizens of high moral character and good standing in your community. It is recommended that the greatest possible secrecy be maintained, both in forming the organization and conducting it. Great care must be taken

by your entire organization at all times that nothing is done by it or any member of it to unnecessarily alarm aliens in this country or cause them any apprehension as to the fair manner in which they will be treated. You will personally administer the oath (of enrollment) to each member you enroll and accept, and at the same time assign to that member a number—enter his number on his enrollment blank, his commission card and on the list you will later forward to this office. You will please use great care in the selection of the Captains, Lieutenants, and members of each Company so that each Company can be depended upon to efficiently handle the work assigned to it. In forming your organization, bear in mind the great variety of investigation that you are likely to be called upon by the Government to make, and make your organization large enough to thoroughly cover every business, manufacturing and other interests in your town that in your opinion should be covered—so that you will be immediately informed of any activity that may prove directly or indirectly unfriendly to the best interests of the Government.

Shortly after their meeting in Washington, A. Bruce Bielaski had provided Briggs with a signed letter of introduction to Bureau personnel:

TO ALL SPECIAL AGENTS AND LOCAL OFFICERS, BUREAU OF INVESTIGATION

This note will introduce you to Mr. A. M. Briggs of Chicago, Illinois, who, with the approval of the Department, is organizing confidentially a volunteer committee or organization of citizens for the purpose of co-operating with the Department in securing information of activities of agents of foreign governments or persons unfriendly to this Government, for the protection of public property, etc.

It will be the aim of such organization to supply to you information and to assist you in securing information as to any matters which you may present to it, and it is planned that some one in the organization will be designated to deal with the agent in charge of this service in each city.

Mr. Briggs understands fully that this arrangement must be kept as confidential as practicable and that great care must be taken that nothing is done by it to unnecessarily alarm aliens in this country or cause them any apprehension as to the fair manner in which they will be treated and that no arrests should be caused except after consultation with the Federal authorities.

Please assist Mr. Briggs in any way practicable and arrange to take advantage of the assistance and co-operation which he may offer through this organization.

As intended, Briggs used Bielaski's note in contacting bureau special agents around the country to obtain their assistance in building the League. In a cover letter that he included with each communiqué, he introduced the agent to the newly appointed chief of the local APL division who would be in contact "as soon as his organization is completed, to place himself under your command for whatever work you may have for this local organization to do in furthering the interests of the government. This movement is being received with great enthusiasm by the agents of the Department throughout the country, as it means the placing under your command of a corps of intelligent men of good standing in the community who will be at all times ready to assist you in any work that you may assign to them." Special agents at field offices across the United States, previously constrained by a lack of personnel and resources, were quick to take advantage of the opportunity for free manpower and provided strong support for the development of local APL branches within their jurisdictions.

The response from businessmen to Briggs's appeal was similarly immediate and enthusiastic. The country was threatened by a powerful foe, and men across the land were swept up in a wave of patriotism, searching for a way to play a part in her defense. Briggs's call was particularly well received by older men unable to join the armed services, and by younger men whose assistance to their country was limited by family obligations. At the time, there were many volunteer organizations being formed to help the war effort in one way or another, but most were independent civic organizations. The American Protective League was operating under the direction of the US Department of Justice and the Bureau of Investigation. This was a powerful attraction to the men being asked to join.

As a result, the growth of the league was meteoric. "Every day saw new men enrolled, big men, men eager to contribute time, money, experience, brains, energy and faithfulness." Within *weeks* 500 men in Chicago had been enrolled as APL members and were soon actively investigating cases. In May 1917, *two months* after Briggs's plan received approval from Bielaski in Washington, there were APL branch divisions located in over 400 cities throughout the country, with a total enrollment of approximately 80,000 members. By mid-July 1917, the League would be established in over 900 US cities and towns, and the total enrollment had grown to about 112,000 men.

The city of Chicago was where the League had originated, and it was here that Briggs, as nominal chief, personally initiated the formation of an American Protective League division. From his circle of business acquaintances he recruited a handful of experienced and capable captains, who in turn established their own working squads. One of the captains that Briggs appointed in Chicago, a friend and fellow advertising man named Charles Daniel Frey, would have an enormous impact on the development and future course of the League.

Charles Daniel Frey was born in Denver, Colorado, on October 9, 1886. He was a gifted artist and, following a public school education, studied art for several years at the Henry Reade School of Art in Denver. Moving to Chicago in 1905, he took a position with the Hearst News Service, and two years later, joined the advertising staff of the *Chicago Evening Post*. In 1912, twenty-five-year-old Frey left the *Post* to strike out on his own, forming the Charles Daniel Frey Company, an advertising agency located on the top floor of Chicago's Monroe Building, which became a great success. Like Briggs, Frey's achievements in advertising brought him wealth and social stature, granting entrance to a number of Chicago clubs and associations. It was during this period that Frey made the acquaintance of A. M. Briggs, who was impressed by the young man's leadership, energy, and organizational ability. In a 1914 letter cordially addressed "My Dear Charles," Briggs informed him that "your fame as a chap who has done things has reached New York and many fellows I have met speak of you in that manner." A later writer would comment "Frey is a genius to my mind—he bristles with ideas all the time. He is the only man I know who can personally plan, lay out, design, and write an advertisement that will bring home the money—from start to finish. And certainly he is the most industrious person I have ever met. He has steam and energy enough to tire out forty strong men."

Just six weeks after appointing him a captain, Briggs promoted the thirty-year-old Frey to the position of chief of the entire Chicago Division. Frey in turn recruited a staff of assistants and chose his business attorney, Victor Elting, as assistant chief. Elting, forty-five years old and a father of three, was a graduate of Columbia University and the law school of the University of Michigan at Ann Arbor. He had built a successful law practice in Chicago and was renowned for his ability to unravel the thorniest legal issues for his clients. For Frey, Elting, and Briggs, League service would become an unsalaried full-time occupation, and their business affairs would be placed in the hands of others for the duration of the war.

Reviewing the organization in Chicago that he now commanded, Frey immediately became aware of a critical problem. Briggs's and Crockett's main focus during the frenzied early months of the League's existence had been to "get things going"—to establish a national organization as quickly as possible with the limited resources at hand. America would soon be at war, and time was of the essence if the League was to protect the country from an anticipated wave of enemy-inspired activity. But instead of a clear plan of organization and standardized methods

of operation, the first APL chiefs had received only vague guidelines regarding how they were to organize their divisions:

> The Chief of each local organization will sub-divide his organ-
> ization into such numerical units as may seem advisable, after
> conference with the local government agent, and appoint a
> captain to command each separate unit of his organization. .
> . . We suggest that your captains be instructed to each enroll a
> company of from 15 to 50 men. . . . In forming your compa-
> nies it is advisable to bear in mind the great variety of investi-
> gation that you are likely to be called upon to make with the
> idea of assigning certain classes of work to each company. . . . The
> local organization Chief will keep in touch with this office
> only in a general way on the activities of his organization,
> rendering only such general reports of their progress as may
> be safely entrusted to the mails.

The lack of a detailed organizational plan resulted in APL investigative members being enrolled without any regard to where
they lived, and the lieutenants and operatives of one captain
being intermixed throughout the territory of other captains.
This made assigning cases and managing their investigation
extremely difficult. It appeared to Frey that allotting cases for
investigation according to the district in which the operative
lived would provide greater efficiency and better results, while
making the operative "the neighborhood expert."

Moving into an office in Room 606 of the Federal Building,
Frey's first priority became a total reorganization of the Chicago
Division's myriad of independent, often overlapping, companies
into a single, efficient intelligence and investigative force. He
began by creating a new organizational hierarchy in which the
functions required to support the League (membership, legal,
finance), as well as the groups engaged in intelligence gathering and investigation, could be efficiently managed by a single
executive leadership team. It would become the standard model
for organization used by American Protective League divisions
nationwide.

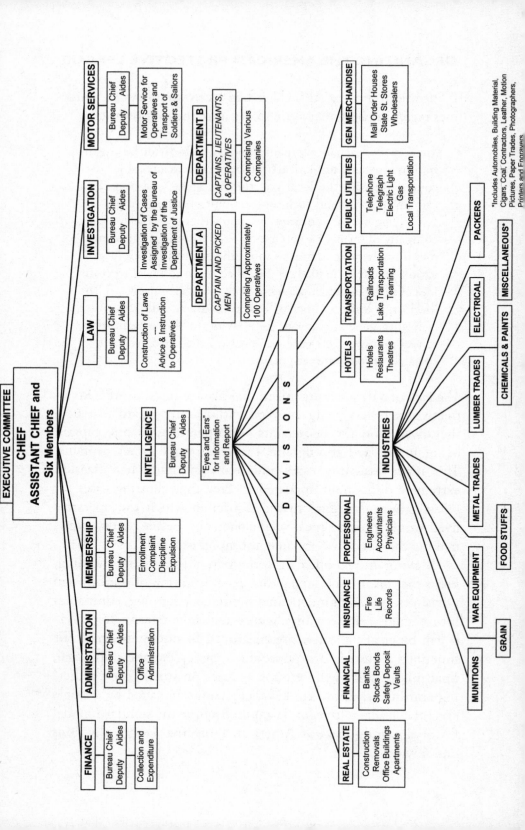

The foundation of the organization was the Bureau of Intelligence. Its secret members would be the "eyes and ears" of the League, quietly gathering evidence for other members to investigate. The Bureau of Intelligence was divided into nine divisions, each under the command of a division chief, and included a "Division of Industries" with a further subdivision containing members in individual plants and offices. The duties of APL members in the Bureau of Intelligence were two-fold: to monitor the activities of thousands of German aliens and potential enemy sympathizers located throughout the key financial and industrial companies in Chicago and to assist operatives and agents in the bureau and the Department of Justice with investigations into banks, insurance companies, and industrial establishments.

Real Estate Division: monitored all activities in the real estate field and provided investigators with information concerning building construction and occupancy and vacancies from office buildings, houses, and apartments.

Financial Division: kept watch over banks, brokerage houses, and safety deposit vaults, furnishing investigators with foreign transaction records and data concerning transactions by alien enemies, including safety deposit use.

Insurance Division: provided information gleaned by insurance inspectors on the character and use of buildings and plants, reports on casualties, and personal insurance data.

Professional Division: included engineers, accountants, physicians, and other professionals. Its members were to supply any information of interest that came their way, as well as provide case-related professional advice needed by investigators. (Physician operatives, for example, could obtain information from any hospitals with which they were connected.)

Opposite page: The American Protective League divisional hierarchy created by Charles Daniel Frey in 1917. It would become the standard model of organization used by League Divisions nationwide.

Hotel Division: reported on activities at hotels, restaurants, and theatres.

Transportation: monitored all shipping, including railroads, trucking, shipping, and teaming (horse-drawn wagons).

Public Utilities Division: covered all utility lines and methods of communication including telephone, telegraph, radio, electricity, gas, and elevated and traction lines.

General Merchandise: monitored activity in retail stores, mail order houses, and all wholesalers.

Industries Division: kept watch over the activities at key industrial plants, such as munitions, war equipment, metal trades, and chemical producing facilities. At each of these plants a captain was appointed, typically an executive officer of the company. He, in turn, would appoint a lieutenant within each department of the facility, who would enlist the required number of operatives.

The Intelligence Bureau provided the American Protective League with a network of spies situated throughout the business world. Its operatives were considered "inactive" APL members, not called upon to investigate cases themselves, just to quietly wait, watch, and report on any matter of interest to the government.

The APL "Bureau of Investigation" was responsible for the investigation of all cases assigned to the League by the Department of Justice. (Author's Note: The APL "Bureau of Investigation" was named after the Department of Justice "Bureau of Investigation" with whom they closely worked, perhaps to suggest the latter organization's professionalism. To avoid confusion in this narrative, the APL unit will be referred to as the "Investigative Bureau" or "IB", while the DOJ entity will be called the "Bureau of Investigation" or "BOI".) It was organized geographically, with members assigned according to their residence. The territory of the division was divided into inspection districts, each under the command of an inspector who reported to the chief. Individual inspection districts were in turn divided into territorial units under the command of a captain. Beneath each captain was a company with a number of platoons, each one under the command of a lieutenant. No platoon was to exceed ten operatives in size.

In the League's Investigative Bureau, quality was preferred over quantity. Cases that were approved for investigation within a district were sent to its inspector, and were then assigned by a captain to the man best qualified based on his location or profession to conduct the investigation. In the organizational plan created for the Chicago Division by Charles Daniel Frey, Chicago's Investigative Bureau was divided in two: Department A and Department B.

Department A was under the command of a department chief and consisted of a squad of men particularly well qualified by experience and ability to conduct important investigations. These men were considered "active" APL members, willing to devote 100 percent of their time, if necessary, to a League investigation. They were also subject to the call of the superintendent of the Justice Department Bureau of Investigation in Chicago for direct assistance as required.

Department B was also under the command of a department chief, but was further divided into a number of companies, each led by a captain. These companies were organized based upon the residential and business location of their members as well as their business occupation. The Investigative Bureau of a League division was expected to establish a close working relationship with the special agent in charge of the local (Justice Department) BOI field office in order to provide the greatest possible assistance to the government. In larger cities it was initially deemed highly desirable that a BOI special agent be assigned to the APL Investigative Bureau to direct its investigations.

Under Frey's plan, five functional support bureaus backed the operations of a league division: Finance, Administration, Membership, Law, and Motor Service.

Finance procured the funds necessary to carry on the work of the division from member initiation fees, and contributions from businesses and private citizens. Members of this bureau also handled all expenditures, which in the case of the Chicago Division were audited by Price, Waterhouse & Company. **Administration** was in charge of office administration, including the distribution of cases and filing of case reports. **Membership** was responsible for enrolling members, and handling complaints, discipline, and expulsions from the league. It included a board that investigated all applications for membership and a trial board that enforced the rules of conduct required of members. Membership also assigned members to their company or department and was responsible for making appointments and promotions. **Law** was composed of attorneys that advised operatives on all legal matters, including applicable laws and proper evidence related to cases. Law attorneys also interrogated suspects, revised the reports of operatives, and prepared them for submission to the BOI. **Motor Service** enlisted members with automobiles to support the transportation needs of the division as well as those of Justice Department investigators. In a day when auto ownership was not universal, this was an important capability.

The operations of an APL division were directed by a chief and assistant chief, often as members of a larger executive or advisory committee. To ensure the greatest cooperation with government agencies and departments, it was considered desirable that members of this committee include the special agent in charge of the BOI field office for the district, the chief of the local police force, representatives of army and navy intelligence, and representatives of other key government organizations. This executive committee completed the organizational framework created by Charles Daniel Frey. As applied in other APL divisions around the country, Frey's plan would vary according to local conditions, such as the size and general character of the community.

When Briggs first proposed the idea for a volunteer citizen force, his modest ambition was to raise several companies of men to support the BOI's investigators. But almost overnight, a nationwide secret army emerged that was as well-organized as any corporate or governmental bureaucracy. Although a ground-swell of patriotism fueled the growth of the American Protective League, it was not a spontaneous "grassroots" organization of local citizens. In a spirit of public service that was typical of the time, individuals from every walk of life voluntarily joined its disciplined ranks, agreeing to submit to direction from the members above them. From the start, the League was a "top down" organization with individual division leaders selected who in turn chose the next rank of members, and so on, until their local organization was complete, all according to Frey's prearranged design. With the desire of each successive leadership level to similarly select supporting members that would help to ensure their success, a highly competent organization typically resulted.

The spirit of patriotism that was generated with the outbreak of war made it an easy matter to secure officers and men of the highest caliber to staff the different bureaus of a League division. After being introduced to the type of work that they would do and the government's pressing need for their service, business and professional men from across the country were quick to answer the call of the American Protective League. The "blue chip" team recruited to leadership positions in Frey's Chicago Division included the following seasoned business, military, and civic leaders:

Executive Committee, Bureau Chiefs, and Intelligence Division Chiefs of the APL Chicago Division.

Executive Committee

- Charles Daniel Frey, Chief   Charles Daniel Frey Company
- Victor Elting, Assistant Chief   Private Attorney
- Hinton G. Clabaugh   Superintendent, Department of Justice

- W. I. Furbershaw — Assistant Superintendent, Department of Justice

- Herman F. Schuettler — Chief of the Chicago Police Department

- Major Thomas B. Crockett — Military Intelligence Division, War Department

- Lieut. Colonel Roger S. Fitch — US Army General Staff, Intelligence, Central Department

- Captain C. S. Cochran — US Naval Intelligence Bureau

Bureau Chiefs

- Bruce D. Smith (Finance) — Vice President, Northern Trust Company

- J. Medlock (Administration) — Price, Waterhouse & Company

- Wallace Heckman (Membership) — Business Director and Counsel, University of Chicago

- L. E. Howard (Motor Service) — Member, Chicago Stock Exchange

- Horace Kent Tenney (Law) — Tenney, Harding & Sherman, Lawyers

- P. J. Barry (Investigation) — Special Agent, Department of Justice Bureau of Investigation

- Howard Elting (Intelligence)   Adams & Elting
  (Past President of the
  Chicago Association
  of Commerce)

Intelligence Division Chiefs

- James B. Forgan (Financial)   President, First
  National Bank
- R. H. Aishton (Transportation) President, Chicago &
  North West Railway
- B. E. Sunny (Public Utilities)   President, Chicago
  Telephone Company
- Robert J. Thorne   President,
  (General Merchandise)   Montgomery Ward &
  Company
- Bion J. Arnold (Professional)   Chairman, Board of
  Supervisory Engineers
  Chicago Traction
  Lines
- T. E. Donnelly (Industries)   R. R. Donnelley &
  Sons
- Don M. McLennan (Insurance) Marsh & McLennan
- Wyllys W. Baird (Real Estate)   Baird & Warner
- John B. Drake (Hotels)   Blackstone Hotel

The Chicago Division would grow to become the largest and best-organized division in the League, with members situated throughout the Chicago business world. At the time of the Armistice, the division's membership totaled 4,500 "active" investigatory members and 7,000 "inactive" members in its "eyes and ears" Intelligence Division. By that time, the division was being assigned 175 cases per day by the Department of

Justice for investigation. During the course of the war, the APL's Chicago Division would conduct over 99,000 investigations for the Department of Justice. The division's operating expenses amounted to approximately $7,000 per month (in 1917-1918 dollars), raised both from its members and from the donations of individuals and businesses. The Chicago Division headquarters employed 66 full-time stenographers and clerks that were directed by 31 staff members, and the division maintained 18 satellite captain's offices. According to Department of Justice Superintendent Clabaugh, "Without exaggeration, I think the Chicago Division of the American Protective League did seventy-five percent of the Government investigatory work (in Chicago) throughout the war. It seems to me this one sentence covers the situation."

The strong support that the Chicago Division provided to the BOI was replicated by hundreds of other League divisions around the country. At its peak, the New York Division had over 4,500 members that covered the Southern and Eastern Federal Districts of New York, extending roughly from Poughkeepsie to Montauk Point. The New York office was maintained by 73 staff members and processed over 70,000 cases. On April 10, 1918, Charles F. DeWoody, the division superintendent of the US Department of Justice in New York, stated, "The American Protective League in this city—in my opinion, ranks with the Bureau of Investigation as the important investigating and prosecuting Bureau. I should say that the American Protective League will be carrying a full 50-50 of the load of the Bureau of Investigation from this time on."

Although difficulties in the relationship between the Bureau of Investigation and the League had occurred early on (particularly with regard to badges that the League issued to its members marked "Secret Service," drawing the ire of the Department of the Treasury, the parent department of the US Secret Service), the American Protective League had proven itself to be a valuable resource for the Justice Department. Until the summer of 1917, the League was only one of a handful of private organizations engaged in volunteer work for the government without official status, but after seeing the results the APL had achieved within a few short months, BOI Chief Bielaski became determined to make the League an official auxiliary of the Department of Justice.

On June 15, 1917, Bielaski called Briggs to a meeting in Washington. The Department would recognize the American Protective League as an official auxiliary and provide the organization with official duties to perform, Bielaski offered, but only if the League agreed to discontinue distributing badges labeled "Secret Service" and notify its members that they were not, in fact, associated in any way with the US Secret Service. It would also be required of all new members to swear an oath to uphold the Constitution of the United States, and to never display their credentials to anyone except League officers or authorized government officials. Finally, a complete list of the officers in every League division would be supplied to the Department of Justice. Briggs quickly acceded to Bielaski's demands, and a short time later the League received official government status.

"The matter of Government recognition is now settled," Briggs wrote to Frey on June 26. "Chief Bielaski this morning definitely approved the enclosed form for use on all letterheads, member's commission cards, enrollment blanks, etc." The document that Briggs attached to his letter for the first time linked the organization's name and that of its government sponsor in a bold heraldic font that publicized their new relationship:

American Protective League

Organized with the Approval and Operating Under the Direction of the United States Department of Justice, Bureau of Investigation

Members of the League would no longer be carrying out assignments as independent volunteers. From now on, they would be acting under the authority of the US Government. When conducting an investigation after receipt of instructions, APL members were authorized to state that they were "securing information for the Department of Justice."

By September 1917, the League had expanded to the point that it far exceeded the capabilities of any one man to lead and direct it. At the same time, the burgeoning war effort was creating ever larger demands for investigatory assistance from both the Justice Department and a host of other government agencies. Communicating with Washington as well as coordinating the activities of over 1,000 League divisions from the Edison Building in Chicago had become an impossible task for Albert Briggs's small team. In reponse, Briggs created a new ruling directorate for the organization and proposed that the APL's central headquarters be moved from Chicago to Washington, DC. The new Board of National Directors would consist of three individuals: Charles Daniel Frey, Victor Elting, and Briggs himself, with each man equal in rank. The chief duties of the board would be to coordinate the activities of the local divisions around the country, to standardize methods of organization and operations of the divisions, to define national policies for the League, and to maintain a point of contact with the Department of Justice and other government agencies. In practice, Briggs's duties would center on organizing new APL divisions around the country and improving the operation of existing ones. Frey would act as the League's liaison to the Military Intelligence Division of the War Department, accepting a captaincy from the US Army. Victor Elting, a skilled lawyer, would be the league's intermediary to the Department of Justice and run the Washington office.

The decision to move the association's National Headquarters from its rent-free offices in the Peoples Gas Building in Chicago to wartime Washington, where space was now at a premium, would prove the more difficult problem. The American Protective League was a self-financed organization, with each division funding its own operations. There was no ready source of cash to finance the move. For a solution, the National Directors turned to the members of the Chicago Division.

Charles Daniel Frey discreetly put out the word that the members of the division were to attend a special evening meeting at the Medinah Temple. Located in North Chicago, the

Medinah Temple had been constructed by Masons in 1912. It was a colossal structure designed to resemble a Middle Eastern palace, with high oval-shaped windows and enormous onion domes atop the two corner towers at its front. Inside the temple was a central meeting room the size of a playing field, surrounded by three levels of stadium seating that could accommodate over 4,000 people. Frey expected twice that number to attend.

On the night chosen for the gathering, without any public notice, League members from across greater Chicago silently converged on the Medinah Temple at the appointed hour. Guards had been posted at the entrances to the building, and admission required the display of an APL member commission card. Soon the temple was packed with an expectant audience of 6,700 APL officers and operatives, a low murmur growing from the assembled businessmen, as in hushed tones they tried to guess the purpose behind the summons.

At once, the crowd grew silent as Charles Daniel Frey rose and walked to the podium. It must have been an overwhelming moment to a man that only a few months earlier was heading a small advertising agency with a handful of employees, and who now stood to address nearly 7,000 of Chicago's most capable businessmen. Referring to a small set of note cards that he held in his hand, Frey began by recounting the League's origins and its achievements to date. "Compare the early days of the League with the settled 'working machine condition' of today," said Frey. "We have 1,270 towns organized and 250,000 members enrolled throughout America from coast to coast. Over 4,600 investigations were conducted in the month of September alone, and 13,000 new cases are now on file. Every two minutes a new investigation is assigned to the Chicago Division by the government. Why hasn't everyone heard of the League's accomplishments? Because it's Washington's policy to keep them out of the newspapers." Recent meetings with federal officials in Washington underscored the extent to which the government had come to rely upon the League, he said, and there was opportunity for the League to play an even greater role in protecting America.

The huge crowd responded with enthusiasm. Frey concluded his speech with an impassioned appeal. "Now is the time for the American Protective League to rise to the next level in becoming a truly national organization by opening a central headquarters in Washington DC at the seat of federal government." He called upon the men to donate the money needed to make the transition.

"To carry on this great work we must have money. Every investigation conducted by the League costs $1 in expenses, which by the way, is ten times less than if conducted by other methods. No man is expected to contribute who has already contributed unless he wants to. No man should contribute if he feels he can't afford to or if his current circumstances do not permit it. But every <u>man</u> who can donate <u>must</u>! The League must be made permanent for the duration of the war. This really is for your protection—your home and your business. This is no time for small ideas or for arguments. It's time for <u>big</u> things and for <u>big</u> ideas. We must raise $100,000 to safeguard the League. We can't stop the work now—*IT MUST GO ON!*"

After the applause had died down, a collection taken from the audience raised $82,000, a princely sum in 1917.

The next day, the National Directors began logistical planning for the move to the nation's capital. Headquarters was to become a clearinghouse for cases from every section of the country. If the New York divisional headquarters, for example, required information on a suspected enemy agent who claimed that he could be cleared by information from New Orleans, Washington, DC, would act as an intermediary. (However, as the various Chiefs became acquainted with each other on a first-name basis, they began to cut corners and send requests directly to their counterparts.) Soon the primary occupation of the National Headquarters was the assignment of cases from federal agencies. Each morning a multitude of government departments and bureaus deluged the headquarters staff with a flood of cases relating to a broad range of activities. These cases would be quickly relayed to the proper APL division and a response sent back to the requesting official.

The League's first headquarters in Washington was at 1537 I Street. It was a modest suite of three offices, with a support staff composed of two stenographers and a file clerk. Briggs, Frey, and Elting, accustomed to a life of comfort, now resided in spartan rooms above their offices, initially without heat or hot water. But in less than a year, the work of the APL had grown to such an extent that they would need to move again, this time to occupy an entire building on H Street, with a clerical staff more than ten times larger, for by then the League had become a powerful secret force in American domestic life.

In May 1917, Chief Bielaski sent a letter to Briggs congratulating him on the early success of the organization:

> I desire to take this opportunity to express to you my appreciation of the very efficient work which the American Protective League is doing in a great many places. The members have been ready and willing, when ever called upon, and have rendered us efficient service. It is a great source of satisfaction to know that we can fall back on this League for assistance should some particular emergency arise.
>
> The future undoubtedly holds a large amount of work of probably a different character than that heretofore undertaken, and we are relying upon the League to help do it when the occasion comes.

But no one could have imagined the endeavors the American Protective League would soon take part in.

CHAPTER 3

BATTLING GERMAN SPIES AND SABOTEURS

Fires and explosions tore across the United States almost as soon as Europe marched to war in 1914. On August 30, 1914, a Du Pont gunpowder mill at Pompton Lakes, New Jersey, blew up. In September, there was an explosion at the Wright Chemical Works, gun cotton factory in Elizabeth, New Jersey, that killed three people and caused extensive damage. In October 1914, munitions works at the Pain Fireworks Display Company in Chicago and the Detwiller & Street Fireworks Company in Jersey City, New Jersey, also exploded, at the combined cost of six lives and tremendous property damage.

These early catastrophes were chalked up as industrial accidents caused by greatly increased demand from Allied forces. But during the first seven months of 1915, "accidents" at munitions plants throughout the United States continued at an ever-increasing pace. The Du Pont powder manufacturing facilities at Haskell, New Jersey, Carney's Point, New Jersey, Wayne, Pennsylvania, and Wilmington, Delaware, all experienced explosions and fires.

On May 3, there was a gun cotton explosion at the Anderson Chemical Company in Wallington, New Jersey, that killed three people. A similar explosion killed five more at the Equitable powder plant at Alton, Illinois. The Buckthorne plant of the John A. Roebling Company, which manufactured artillery shell components at Trenton, New Jersey, was completely destroyed by fire, the loss estimated at $1.5 million. A dynamite barge in the Seattle harbor exploded on May 30, with an earthquake-level shock wave that caused horrific damage to the area. On June 26, a chemical explosion at the Aetna powder plant in Pittsburgh killed one man and seriously injured ten others.

During this period before America's entry into the war, the source of ignition for many of these unexplained fires and explosions could be found in the German embassy in Washington. There, the German ambassador to the United States, Count Johann von Bernstorff, the scion of several generations of diplomats, utilized his charm and social skills to try to win American support for the German position—or at a minimum, to maintain America as a neutral on the sidelines. But an assignment of equal importance from Berlin tasked von Bernstorff with doing everything in his power to stem the flow of war supplies from the United States to the Allies.

In November 1914, von Bernstorff received a communiqué signed by Dr. Fischer, councillor general of the German army, that began: "Enclosed is the circular of November 22, 1914 for information and execution upon United States territory. We draw your attention to the possibility of recruiting destroying agents among anarchist labor organizations." It further notified von Bernstorff that sums would be made available for recruiting agents to destroy factories and war stocks in America.

In the same month, a circular from German Naval Headquarters was dispatched to the embassy:

> It is indispensable by the intermediary of the third person having no relation with the official representatives of Germany to recruit progressively agents to organize explosions on ships

sailing to enemy countries in order to cause delays and confusion in the loading, the departure, and the unloading of these ships. With this end in view, we particularly recommend to your attention the deckhands, among whom are to be found a great many anarchists and escaped criminals. The necessary sums for buying and hiring persons charged with executing the projects will be put at your disposal on your demand.

Also at Ambassador von Bernstorff's disposal were three ready subordinates at the embassy. Dr. Heinrich Albert was the money man. American banks had granted Albert millions of dollars in loans, and he had personally raised millions more by selling short-term German notes to American investors. Through Albert, von Bernstorff now had a small fortune at hand to finance schemes aimed at disrupting the supply shipments. Franz von Papen, von Berstorff's dueling-scarred military attaché, was a cavalry officer who had likewise become obsessed with stopping the flow of Allied supplies. He would direct an army of spies and saboteurs throughout the United States and Canada. The embassy's naval attaché, the well-cultivated and charming Karl Boy-Ed, had originally been dispatched by the Kriegsmarine to America to study the US Navy—its ships, personnel, strategy, and plans for expansion. With the outbreak of the war in Europe however, Boy-Ed's duties had been similarly redirected to espionage and sabotage. He cultivated contacts among the German sailors that had been interned since the outbreak of the war, obtaining information about ships and cargos bound for England and France. Like von Papen, Boy-Ed maintained a corps of German reservists and agents prepared to take action against the Allied shipments.

These four men and a handful of willing accomplices now embarked on a series of plots and subterfuges in support of the German war effort. Making use of intelligence agent Horst von der Goltz, von Papen backed a plan to blow up the Welland Canal that linked Lake Ontario to Lake Erie in Canada. A team sent there with a charge of dynamite only aborted the mission when it became obvious to the party that the canal was too well guarded. A counterfeiting operation was set up in Manhattan to forge American passports for the thousands of German reserve officers stranded in the United States, to enable them to return to Germany and participate in the war. After repatriating scores of reservists, the forging organization was infiltrated by Justice Department agents and rapidly disintegrated. The embassy group also backed various plots to recruit Indian Hindus and Irish nationals for sabotage missions in the United States, as well as to mount revolutionary diversions in their homelands.

To assist in the sabotage program, von Papen obtained the services of Paul Koenig, the hulking superintendent of detectives for the Atlas Line, a subsidiary of the Hamburg-American Steamship Line. Koenig was well-known along the waterfront, where he was in equal parts loathed and feared. Koenig formed a clandestine organization of spies, reservists, German-Americans, and assorted riff-raff that became a virtual action force at the disposal of embassy officials. Koenig supplemented his wages with payments for the work he carried out for the embassy, and kept a detailed book of accounts of each job that included the name of the person assigned and the costs incurred. Participants were given a two-character code name in Koenig's journal; assignments were similarly coded, with each sabotage mission being designated a "D-case."

During the latter half of 1915, the wave of suspicious explosions and fires continued unabated at American munitions plants. There were incendiary fires at the Midvale Steel Company and the artillery shell plant of the Brill Car Company both located in Philadelphia, and another in the artillery shell department of the Diamond Forge and Steel Company in Pittsburg. In August, a powder flash explosion killed ten men at the Bethlehem Steel Company in Bethlehem, Pennsylvania. At the Newport News Navy Yard, there were three fires in three weeks. In September, an explosion occurred at the Curtiss Aircraft factory, there was another at the National Cable and Conduit Company's artillery shell factory in Hastings, New York, and an explosion killed two men at an artillery shell factory in Pittsburgh owned by Westinghouse Electric. A fire at the Bethlehem Steel plant on November 10 destroyed 800 artillery guns.

The perpetrators carried out their work at night, usually during the weekend when the munition plants were closed, to lessen the chance of being detected and limit the loss in innocent life. They were mindful of the impact that discovery of their action could have on US public opinion, and civilian casualties would make the fallout from any incident that much greater. Sometimes plant watchmen were paid to be "less watchful" on the night slated for sabotage to help ensure their escape. The saboteurs took great care to leave no traceable evidence of the cause of the "accident," common factory items like rags and cleaning solvents at times being used to trigger the combustion and munitions stored at the plant providing the explosive force. Despite these precautions, by the end of 1915 the sheer number of unexplained incidents (37 US munition plants damaged or destroyed at an estimated loss of $6 million) was making it clear to both investigators and the press alike that a criminal plot was behind the destruction. As one reporter noted: "Inquiry throughout the East and Middle West reveals that there were exceedingly few fires or explosions a year ago in the plants which have suffered most recently. Federal and other authorities have been working hard on the suspicion that these depredations were the work of conspirators, but if they were, their organization has been so complete that the officials have as yet been unable to round up the plotters. The greater part of these depredations against property—if such they were—were committed in the states adjacent to New York and many in the Metropolitan area." Even without physical evidence, there was now strong suspicion of German involvement.

Recognizing the need to establish a sabotage capability independent of the highly visible (and therefore highly vulnerable) embassy group, in March 1915 a captain in the German Navy, Franz von Rintelen was dispatched to America. Soon to be renowned as "the Dark Invader," Captain von Rintelen's first assignment was to create a disguised company and enter into large purchase contracts with US munitions manufacturers, thereby denying ammunition to the Allied purchasing agents. Before departing Germany, von Rintelen outlined his plans in conferences at the German war office, the foreign office, and the finance ministry, concluding each presentation with the statement: "Ich kaufe was ich kann; alles andere schlage ich kaput!"— "I'll buy up what I can and blow up what I can't!"

Although he had been empowered to raise a vast amount of money to carry out the scheme (a $500,000 cable transfer had been made for him as starters), upon his arrival von Rintelen learned that the production capacity of the United States was now so great that it would be impossible for any purchases that he would make, no matter the size, to cause even a momentary delay in supplies reaching the Allied powers. The "Dark Invader" would need to find another way to impede the flow of munitions.

The solution came when a German chemist named Dr. Scheele paid a surprise visit. Sent to von Rintelen by Franz von Papen, Dr. Scheele had developed a startling new invention for sabotage. It was a cigar-shaped hollow lead tube with a copper disk at the center dividing the tube into two chambers. One side would be filled with picric acid, and the other with sulphuric acid. Plugs inserted at either end would seal the device. When the acids ate through the copper disk and combined together, the resulting combustion sent a huge stream of flame out of the ends of the tube. Varying the thickness of the copper disk would adjust the time delay before ignition.

After hearing Dr. Scheele's proposal, Von Rintelen leaned back in his chair wide-eyed as he considered the potential for using the deadly devices in sabotaging Allied munitions ships. Dr. Scheele's "cigars" could be smuggled onboard by interned German seamen or ordinary deckhands and left to ignite when the ships were far out to sea with no risk to the agent that had placed them. "Fabelhafte!" Von Rintelen arranged for a large quantity to be manufactured in the workshop of a German Lloyd liner, the *Friedriche der Grosse,* that was interned at Hoboken, New Jersey.

Dr. Scheele's "cigars" opened a new front in Germany's clandestine war in peacetime America. Soon accounts of sabotage activity on freighters carrying Allied war material became as frequent in the *Shipping News* as munitions plant fires had become in the daily newspapers:

- April 29, 1915—Cressington afire at sea
- May 2—Kirk Oswald, bomb found on board
- May 8—Bankdale, two bombs found in cargo
- May 13—Samland, afire at sea
- May 21—Anglo-Saxon, bomb found on board
- June 2—Strathway, afire at sea
- July 4—Minnehaha, bomb exploded at sea
- July 13—Touraine, afire at sea
- July 14—Lord Downshire, afire
- July 20—Knutford, fire in hold
- July 24—Craigside, five fires in hold
- July 27—Arabic, two bombs found on board
- August 9—Asuncion de Larrinaga, afire at sea
- August 13—Williston, bombs in cargo
- August 27—Dixie, fire while loading

Even if the target vessel did not explode or become so fire-damaged that it could not complete its voyage, the ship's captain would often flood the hold containing munitions to eliminate the chance of an explosion, thereby destroying the war material in the process. To orchestrate the placement of the incendiary bombs, Von Rintelen acquired the services of Frederick Hinsch, a tough but clever North German Lloyd steamer captain. Hinsch was well-known among the interned German sailors living along the Baltimore waterfront, and he eagerly recruited them to place the deadly devices on ships bound for England and France.

Germany's campaign to disrupt arms shipments to the Allies had enjoyed great success during this early phase of the war, but a significant lapse in 1915 resulted in the undoing of several key players. On the afternoon of July 24, Dr. Albert, the German commercial attaché, and George Sylvester Viereck, editor of a German language newspaper called *The Fatherland,* boarded an elevated train in Lower Manhattan. Unbeknownst to the Germans, two US Secret Service agents shadowing Viereck for suspected violation of American neutrality laws, also boarded the train and kept the pair under a watchful eye. Viereck eventually departed the train at his stop, followed by one of the Secret Service agents, while Albert remained on board. The train rumbled along the track under the hot July sun, and Albert began to slumber in his seat. He soon awoke with a start to discover that the train had reached his stop, and he quickly rushed off leaving his briefcase behind. Instantly realizing his mistake, Albert hopped back aboard the train only to discover that the briefcase was gone—snatched by the quick-witted Secret Service agent. When the contents of the briefcase were examined by government officials, they proved to be a revelation, outlining a variety of German schemes to disrupt war shipments from US companies. At the direction of the White House, the documents were leaked to the *New York World,* which published them in a spectacular series of articles.

The circulation of Albert's secret documents in the newspapers and the realization that several US police agencies were now hot on his trail brought von Rintelen to the conclusion that the time had come to return to Germany. Booking passage on the Holland-American liner *Noordam* under an assumed name, von Rintelen got as far as Dover before being arrested by English authorities, who were fully aware of his activities from decoded German message intercepts.

In October 1915, a German army lieutenant named Robert Fay, engaged in the early phases of a sabotage operation in New Jersey, was also arrested. During his interrogation, Fay named von Papen as a co-conspirator. In December, New York police arrested Paul Koenig, the German shipping line detective. Searching Koenig's room, they discovered a number of incriminating documents, including his book of accounts listing all of the "D-case" sabotage projects he had organized. Based upon the weight of evidence against the German diplomats, US Secretary of State Lansing demanded that both attachés, Franz von Papen and Karl Boy-Ed, be recalled by their government. Count von Bernstorff, who had not been compromised by any of his subordinate's activities, retained his position as ambassador to the United States.

Despite these setbacks, other German agents such as Captain Hinsch, the North German Lloyd steamer captain, quickly stepped in to fill the void left by the departure of von Rintelen, von Papen, and Boy-Ed. Aware that the movement of Allied troops, artillery, and materiel was heavily dependent on horses and mules from America, German army intelligence devised a ruthless scheme to disrupt their supply. A young German-American doctor named Anton Dilger was dispatched to the United States with a hidden cache of deadly glanders and anthrax germ cultures.

Dilger established a secret laboratory in Maryland where he utilized a bacteria incubator and banks of petri dishes filled with culture media to propagate the lethal germs into a large reserve. Hinsch, in turn, instructed the foreman of his stevedore crews to recruit a handful of reliable men to deliver the germs by surreptitiously inoculating draft horses and mules bound for Europe. Purposefully walking past the dormant animals in their holding pens, the dockworkers would discreetly jab them with hypodermic needles filled with the germ-laden liquid. Within weeks the first symptoms appeared—staggering, convulsions, skin ulcerations—as the bacteria multiplied inside the unfortunate beasts, and death followed shortly thereafter.

While the Allies' supply of draft animals was under covert attack, the swath of destruction at US war plants and munitions facilities continued unabated, with total losses due to suspicious fires and explosions in 1916 actually exceeding those in 1915. The biggest of them all, the crowning achievement of the German sabotage system in America during World War I (and probably the largest explosion in US history up to that time), was the destruction of the munitions depot on Black Tom Island, located off the Jersey shore of New York harbor. Black Tom, so named for its tomcat shape, was the transit point for all Allied munitions transported to Europe. Ammunition arrived at Black Tom by the trainload from around the country, where it was unloaded before being transferred onto freighters bound for Europe.

On July 30, 1916, at 2:08 a.m. exactly (based on the time when hundreds of clocks in the surrounding area stopped working), an enormous blast occurred from the ignition of 2 million pounds of ammunition that was felt as far away as Lancaster, Pennsylvania, 158 miles distant. The explosion shattered

The spectacular munitions explosion perpetrated by German agents at Black Tom Island in New York harbor captured newspaper headlines across the country.

thousands of windows in Lower Manhattan, Brooklyn, and Jersey City. In fact, so many panes of glass were broken by the explosion that there was insufficient plate glass available in the area to repair the damage. The Statue of Liberty was bombarded with shrapnel, its main door, made of iron and weighing almost a ton, was blown off its hinges. Of the twenty-five ammunition storage houses that stretched along a mile of Black Tom Island, only four were still standing after the explosion. Losses included $5 million worth of ammunition, a small fleet of ammunition barges, and over $100,000 worth of plate glass windows. Miraculously, only five people were killed in the blast, but the total material loss was estimated (in 1916 dollars) at $20 million. The destruction of Black Tom by German saboteurs was almost the perfect crime. It was believed at the time that the explosion had been caused by improper handling and storage of ammunition. Not until 1939 would an international commission determine that German agents were actually responsible for the carnage.

When the United States declared war against Germany on April 6, 1917, the German embassy in Washington was closed. Its diplomatic staff returned to Germany, including Ambassador von Bernstorff, who would soon be reassigned to the German embassy in Constantinople. With the outbreak of hostilities, sabotage was now a capital offense. Most of the seasoned German agents—men like Hinsch and Dilger—left the country for the comparative safety of Mexico. Other enemy agents remained, however, and in the company of thousands of potential domestic saboteurs became the target of government investigators, including those of the Justice Department's Bureau of Investigation and its new auxiliary, the American Protective League.

From its inception, a major source of funding for local League divisions was donations solicited from private companies. Much of this revenue came from owners of large industrial concerns—manufacturers, public utilities, mines, and mills that saw themselves as a potential target of "dynamite outrages" perpetrated by German saboteurs or domestic anarchists. These

businessmen wrote regular monthly checks to the League, sub-
sidizing the continued presence of APL members within their
organizations, as supplemental protection to their own plant
security. At some firms, the League's presence actually displaced
the company security force. "One of the largest gas mask factories in the country, employing more than ten thousand persons,
learned of the clever work members of the League were doing.
They induced an APL lieutenant to take over the plant's intelligence system and to remodel it on League lines. He recruited
his operatives from APL men. The innovation was an emphatic
success."

The American Protective League's principal means to counter the threat of German sabotage activities were the Industrial
Divisions, the eyes and ears of the League, that were formed
throughout the chief war plants in each city. A good example is provided by the APL industrial organization in Detroit,
Michigan. During World War I, Detroit's many large auto-
motive, metalworking, and electrical products manufacturers
received over $400 million in contracts for war equipment and
munitions. With this tremendous increase in production, the
amount of ship traffic from the Great Lakes that passed through
the Detroit River became greater than that crossing either the
Suez or Panama Canals. As a combined industrial and transportation hub, Detroit was a prime target for sabotage. Yet no
major destructive act was recorded in Detroit during the entire
period of the war. This achievement was in part attributed to
the APL members at work in factories throughout the Detroit
region.

The American Protective League's Detroit operations began
in the spring of 1917. At first, the division was subsidized solely
by the one dollar initiation fee paid by individual members,
but it soon became clear that effective operations could not
be maintained in Detroit without a stronger financial base. In
December, a meeting of prominent Detroit area manufacturers
was held, resulting in an agreement to provide the APL with
better facilities and improved financial support. A committee of

Detroit businessmen then traveled to Washington to meet with the attorney general. The League's new offices were established in close proximity to Department of Justice's in Detroit shortly thereafter.

Fred Randall, the first chief of the Detroit APL, resigned in March 1918 and was replaced by Frank H. Croul, the city's former police commissioner. Frank Croul's responsibilities as chief of the Detroit APL were then expanded to include not only Detroit, but all of Wayne County, and he immediately got to work reorganizing the operation. Since Detroit businesses had received such a huge volume of war contracts, a separate division was organized under the name, "Plants Protection Department." Operatives were recruited within each factory to serve under the leadership of an APL captain. The plant captain supervised the activities of the APL member workmen and reported directly to the Plants Protection Department at the League headquarters in Detroit. A number of attempts to blow up Detroit business facilities were thwarted by this organization, and it was not unusual for an employee brought into the League office for suspicious activity to be turned over later to the Justice Department or the district attorney's office for prosecution.

One of the industrial concerns under the diligent watch of the American Protective League in Detroit was the Ford Motor Company. At that time, the Ford plant was located in Highland Park, which adjoined the northern boundary of Detroit. An enormous complex of four- and six-story buildings with a combined manufacturing and assembly floor space of forty-five acres, it housed the most modern machine tools and assembly line in the world, and was manned by some of the best engineers and manufacturing personnel in the country. During World War I, the US War Department contracted with Ford to produce 15,000 three-ton tanks, 60 subchaser Eagle Boats, 39,000 Model T transport vehicles, 5,000 Liberty aircraft engines, as well as 415,000 Liberty engine cylinders for use in production by other manufacturers. America's chief contribution to the war in the air was the Liberty aircraft engine.

Throughout the First World War, the Ford plant was under constant threat of sabotage. As Benedict Crowell, assistant secretary of war, noted in the official record of US munitions production, "America's Munitions 1917–1918":

> It was surprising to what extent unfriendly influence in the United States, much of it probably of a pro-German character, cut a figure in the situation. This was particularly true in the supply factories furnishing tools to the Liberty engine plants. Approximately 85 per cent of the tools first delivered for this work were found to be inaccurate and incorrect. These had to be remade before they could be used. Such tools as were delivered to the Liberty plants would mysteriously disappear, or vital equipment would be injured in unusual ways; in several instances cans of explosives were found in the coal at power plants; fire-extinguishing apparatus was discovered to be rendered useless by acts of depredation; and from numerous other evidences the builders of Liberty engines were aware that the enemy had his agents in their plants.

Henry Ford responded to this threat in a number of ways, chief among them being to encourage the American Protective League to organize and operate within the Ford factories. Like other prominent Detroit businessmen, Ford also provided funding to the League and allowed some of his best men to become officers in the organization. The APL captain at the Ford Motor Company was Edwin C. Clemett, the assistant director of the Ford Educational Department, who had 400 APL operatives and lieutenants under his command. Clemett's instructions to these operatives were simple: "Go about your job as you always have—but keep your eyes and ears open for any suspicious action or talk by other employees." APL surveillance of the Ford plant was all-encompassing. According to Clemett, "There were tentacles of the APL organization reaching into every department." Clemett's League duties included interviewing all men of German nativity to determine whether it was safe to allow them to work in factory buildings where munitions were being manufactured." As a result of these interviews, thirty-five men were refused permits to work in the munitions areas.

Although part of the contractual agreement with the government held that any man engaged in war work could be removed at the government's request, this rarely occurred at the Ford plant. It was the company's belief that the safety of the country would be better ensured if a suspected man was moved to another position where he could be closely monitored, rather than be discharged from the Ford plant and potentially go on to commit sabotage at another company. When Clemett and his lieutenants at the Ford plant suspected that an employee might be a risk, the standard procedure was for an operative to be assigned to work on the same bench as the suspected worker. This was called "the interior organization system" by the army's military intelligence division, with which the APL closely worked. One Ford employee named Bittman, who was employed in the tool design room, came under suspicion using the system and was found to have plans for the entire department in his possession when he was caught. He was subsequently interned by the government. The work of the secret APL operatives at the Ford Motor Company resulted in confidential reports on 500 of the 30,000 workers employed at the Ford plant. These reports were sent to the League headquarters in Detroit, as well as to the Department of Justice in Detroit and the army's military intelligence division in Washington. American Protective League surveillance of the Ford facilities helped to ensure that war production at the plant was never disrupted throughout the course of the war.

To protect the war materials being transported along the Detroit River from sabotage, the League instituted its own security system on the waterway. Operatives boarded every ship bound in either direction and examined the credentials of every person on board. If a passenger or ship hand could not produce satisfactory identification they could still continue on the voyage, provided the captain personally guaranteed their character and intentions. But if there was any doubt, the League would wire ahead to other stations along the river to determine whether the man was wanted. Several individuals were captured from ships working the river based on information provided by the Detroit APL.

Apart from the surveillance mounted by the League within war plants and the special precautions taken to protect likely targets, potential sabotage was also thwarted by APL operatives following up on tips provided by the public: thousands of hours of investigatory work spent following up leads, knocking on neighborhood doors, and asking questions.

One investigation began when a tip was received at League headquarters in Chicago regarding the suspicious activities of a man living in District 13. A lieutenant and an operative were dispatched to the rooming house where the man lived. Finding the suspect's room empty, the pair made a thorough search of the premises, finding only a few bags of clothing and a suitcase containing bottles of chemicals. When the subject returned, they questioned him and asked to see his draft registration card. The draft card was correct, but they noticed that his draft board status was listed on the card as "Class Five—Austrian." The pair returned to headquarters to report their findings. When they later went back to the rooming house to question the man further, his room was empty—the Austrian had fled.

Employing a standard tactic of police detectives, the APL men contacted all of the taxicab companies serving the neighborhood and requested they check their records for any recent hires from the rooming house address. They quickly discovered that he had engaged a yellow cab to move to a new address several miles away. Contacting the Chicago police, a raid was organized, and a team of four League members and two Chicago police detectives drove to the man's new lodging and surrounded the building. The Austrian was captured (in disguise) on a third-floor landing while attempting to leap across to another building. Subsequent analysis of the chemicals found in the man's suitcase revealed that they could be used to manufacture enough explosives to blow up a good-sized building. Additional information about the Austrian was received from the New York APL, which substantiated that the man was indeed a dangerous enemy alien.

Another APL investigation began when a traveling salesman passing through Chicago overheard two small children talking. "We have a fine piano in our flat," said the little girl to her playmate. "That's nothing," replied her friend, a small boy, "we've got a German spy in ours." The salesman dutifully reported the exchange to the Department of Justice, and a complaint was forwarded to the American Protective League for investigation. The Chicago headquarters assigned an operative to the case, who began by questioning children in the neighborhood. Soon the operative learned where the boy lived.

Using the pretext that he was working to update the listings in the Chicago City Directory, he asked the landlady of the building where the boy lived for the names and occupations of her tenants. The operative noted that one of the names was German. He was able to gain entry to the German's vacant flat and began a search of the premises. Opening a steamer trunk on the floor, he found a worn cartridge belt filled with ammunition resting on top of a pile of clothes. Rummaging around beneath the clothing, he discovered a well-oiled German Luger pistol, its blued finish gleaming in the daylight, and engineering drawings of the Chicago Municipal Pier and the Federal Building. After replacing the items exactly as he'd found them, the operative questioned the landlady about her German tenant and learned that he worked as a draftsman at the Federal Building.

The next morning, just before sunrise, a team of special agents from the Bureau of Investigation arrested the man, who turned out to be an enemy alien employed by the German government. The man was eventually sent to Leavenworth Penitentiary under an order of internment.

Unlike the large war plants like Ford Motor Company that maintained their own league detachment, smaller shops and factories were given a telephone number to call to report suspicious activity. Manning the phone would be an Industrial Division operative employed in their line of business. An espionage case in New York started with a tip phoned in to division headquarters about electrical parts.

The case began at a small and dingy but extremely busy electrical supply house on the outskirts of the Empire City. Due to the war, business had been good at the shop, the only difficulty being obtaining enough goods to satisfy the growing demand from companies and individuals for wireless components. The electrical store was a two-man operation, consisting of the owner and his sales clerk, a teenager named Simon Rosenstein. Simon was a new employee, but he was also a fast learner and under his boss's expert tutelage soon knew everything there was to know about the products they carried—including components that could only be sold to customers who provided a special permit. Those items the owner told Simon to try to sell on credit, "for with credit, there must be definite knowledge about who is making the purchase."

Early one afternoon, after his boss had departed on an errand and left Simon in charge, a customer entered the shop and began to browse casually through the products on display. He looked no different from anyone else who had visited the shop that day. Thinking that the man was in search of nothing more exciting than a dry cell battery for his front door bell, Simon was surprised when he suddenly began to ask about components that were not on display.

"Do you have any Ruhmkorff coils?" the man inquired.

Simon eyed the man closely. The Ruhmkorff coil was a key component used in building a "spark gap" radio transmitter for sending wireless messages.

"Why no, I don't believe that we have any on hand," he replied.

"I'll pay cash for a Ruhmkorff coil," the man said. Staring at the youth intently, he added, "and there would be an extra $50 in it for you."

"Gee whiz," Simon responded in genuine astonishment, "Honest, we haven't got any of them in stock right now. But I can get you one—this afternoon."

The man smiled. "The instant you hand it over the money is yours."

"There's only one problem—I can't be seen taking extra money in the shop. It would mean losing my job if my boss found out."

The man frowned.

"But I can get away at about 3 o'clock and bring you a Ruhmkorff coil myself," Simon continued, "How about that?"

A look of relief came to the man's face. "That would be fine." He gave the boy an address to bring the coil. "My name is on the door—Mr. Hermann. I'll be waiting for you."

They shook hands and Simon cheerfully watched him exit the shop. As soon as he was certain that Hermann was out of the vicinity, Simon rushed to the telephone and placed a call to a phone number that his boss had required him to memorize. He repeated the number twice to Central to make sure that the operator had gotten it right. When the call was finally put through, Simon asked for a name that he had also been told to memorize.

"That's me," said the voice at the other end of the line.

"There was a guy in our shop a little while ago who was looking to buy a Ruhmkorff coil," said Simon. "that's used in—"

"I know what it's used for," the voice interrupted. "What did he look like? Did you get his name and address?"

After Simon had provided the details of what had transpired, the Electrical Squad operative quickly rang off. "So long old man. We'll be in touch."

The Department of Justice was contacted, and ten minutes later a BOI special agent met the League operative at Hermann's flat. They quickly searched the suspect's room, finding enough evidence to take Hermann into custody when he returned for his appointment with the sales clerk. Following Hermann's arrest, Simon Rosenstein became a hero at the APL's New York headquarters, where he received the personal thanks of Chief Rushmore.

With the United States now on a war footing and American Protective League divisions organizing across the country, destructive acts by German agents and those sympathetic to their cause dwindled rapidly. The days of unchecked sabotage activity by the von Papens, von Rintelens, and Koenigs had come to an end. But in the meantime, another challenge to America's war program had arisen from a different quarter. The American Protective League would now go to war against the Industrial Workers of the World—"the Wobblies."

CHAPTER 4

AT WAR WITH THE WOBBLIES

It was an enormous crowd. Hundreds of men in hard-worn hats and overcoats stood shoulder-to-shoulder in a muddy field, squinting against the early morning sun. Some held hand-lettered signs above their heads. Most of them had traveled a considerable distance to come to this place. As the minutes ticked by, they continued to stand there, patiently waiting in stoic silence. Finally a tall, heavy-set man made his way to the make-shift podium and began to speak.

"Fellow workers . . ." he called out in a booming voice. Immediately a roar erupted from the crowd. The speaker pounded a chunk of wood on the podium to call them to order. "The working class and the employing class have nothing in common. There can be no peace as long as hunger and want are found among millions of working people and the few who make up the employing class have all the good things of life.

"Between these two classes a struggle must go on until the workers of the world organize as a class, take possession of the earth and the machinery of production, and abolish the wage system. Instead of the conservative motto, 'A fair day's wage for a fair day's work,' we must inscribe on our banner the revolutionary watchword: 'Abolition of the wage system.'

"It is the historic mission of the working class to do away with capitalism. The army of production must be organized, not only for the every-day struggle with capitalists, but also to carry on production when capitalism shall have been overthrown. By organizing industrially, we are forming the structure of the new society within the shell of the old."

The crowd roared its approval at hearing the familiar words of their organization's preamble, which most of them could recite by heart. In this year of 1917, the words would have been equally well received at a meeting of Bolsheviks in Russia (at this point on the eve of revolution), but this was America, and a gathering of the Industrial Workers of the World, the "Wobblies." An APL operative in the crowd posing as a reporter quietly opened a small black notebook, and with pencil in hand, began to carefully transcribe every word that the man said, as well as the statements made by each successive speaker . . .

Part trade union, part revolutionary movement, the Industrial Workers of the World was founded in 1905 in Chicago, as a response to the extreme economic inequities that existed in the United States at the turn of the twentieth century. Industrial and agricultural production had grown at a staggering pace during the previous two decades. Major industries like steel, oil, and transportation were controlled by monopolies—"trusts" that were de facto unregulated. The industrial barons that ran these trusts set the market price for their products, as well as employee wages, working conditions, and work schedules. At the same time, in many industries, life had never been worse for the average American worker. Whether in the grain fields of the Midwest, the mineral mines of the Southwest, the lumber forests of the Northwest, or the textile mills of the East, laborers typically worked ten to twelve hours a day for subsistence wages (or less) in dismal and often dangerous working environments. The IWW's goal was to counter the power of the trusts with the power of "one big union," a labor collective that would force decent wages, improve working conditions, and eventually spearhead the overthrow of capitalism by the working class.

The IWW movement grew rapidly, and by 1917 it boasted over 100,000 members. Many of the Wobblies were unskilled migratory workers that traveled from job to job, never setting root or remaining long enough to be considered an ongoing IWW member, so actual membership in the organization was probably far higher. Some have estimated that as many as one million workers were members of the IWW between 1905 and 1917, whether they paid dues or not. Many of these individuals flocked to the IWW's "one big union" because they would have otherwise had no financial or political power. Unusual for the time, the Wobblies accepted anyone regardless of race, religion, or gender: women, migrants, alien immigrants, and, in many areas of the country, black workers. These were people who couldn't vote. Even among those in the population who could vote, economic and social conditions had driven many toward the support of radical candidates. In the 1912 presidential election, the Socialist Party candidate for president, Eugene V. Debs, captured over 900,000 votes (6 percent of the popular vote). In some states, Debs actually won more votes than the Republican presidential candidate. The people's revolution that the Socialists hoped to achieve at the polling place was the same that the IWW hoped to achieve in the workplace.

The uncompromising stance of the Industrial Workers of the World in dealing with management (refusing to recognize contracts, which eliminated mediation as a solution to workplace problems) confronted by employers that took an equally hard line, led to strikes that often resulted in violence and arrests. The tactics employed by the Wobblies are best described in a popular IWW pamphlet of the time, *The IWW: Its History, Structure, and Methods*, which was written by Vincent St. John, one of the organization's early leaders:

> As a revolutionary the Industrial Workers of the World aims to use any and all tactics that will get the results sought with the

least expenditure of time and energy. The tactics used are determined solely by the power of the organization to make good in their use. The question of 'right or wrong' does not concern us.

No terms made with an employer are final. All peace so long as the wage system lasts, is but an armed truce. At any favorable opportunity the struggle for more control of industry is renewed.

No part of the organization is allowed to enter into time contracts with the employers. Where strikes are used, it aims to paralyze all branches of the industry involved, when the employers can least afford a cessation of work—during the busy season and when there are rush orders to be filled.

The Industrial Workers of the World maintains that nothing will be conceded by the employers except that which we have the power to take and hold by the strength of our organization. Therefore we seek no agreements with the employers.

Failing to force concessions from the employers by strike, work is resumed and 'sabotage' is used to force the employers to concede the demand of the workers.

During strikes the works are closely picketed and every effort made to keep the employers from getting workers into the shops. All supplies are cut off from strike bound shops. All shipments are refused or missent, delayed and lost if possible. Strike breakers are also isolated to the full extent of the power of the organization. Interference by the government is resented by open violation of the government's orders, going to jail en masse, causing expense to the taxpayers—which is but another name for the employing class.

In short, the IWW advocates the use of militant 'direct action' tactics to the full extent of our power to make good.

By "direct action tactics," St. John meant any action taken by IWW members at the point of production to obtain concessions. Direct action could mean strikes, demonstrations, boycotts—or sabotage. Walker C. Smith, the editor of the Wobbly journal *Industrial Worker*, described "sabotage" to his readers as:

[. . .] the destruction of profits to gain a revolutionary, economic end. It has many forms. It may mean the damaging of raw materials destined for a scab factory or shop. It may mean the spoiling of a finished product. It may mean the displacement of parts of machinery or the disarrangement of a whole machine where that machine is the one upon which the other machines are dependent for material. It may mean working slow. It may mean poor work. . . . In fact, it has as many variations as there are different lines of work. . . . In case of war, which every intelligent worker knows are whole-sale murders of workers to enrich the master class, there is no weapon so forceful to defeat the employers as sabotage by the rebellious workers in the two warring countries. Sabotage will put a stop to war when resolutions, parliamentary appeals and even a call for general refusal to serve are impotent. But as stated before, sabotage is but one phase of the question. Anti-military and anti-patriotic agitation must also be carried on.

In "Sabotage," a pamphlet printed by the IWW's Cleveland Publishing Bureau, Elizabeth Gurley Flynn, a leading figure during the early years of the IWW movement, commented: "I am not going to attempt to justify sabotage on any moral ground. If the workers consider that sabotage is necessary, that in itself makes sabotage moral. Its necessity is its excuse for existence. And for us to discuss the morality of sabotage would be as absurd as to discuss the morality of the strike or the morality of class struggle itself."

When war broke out in Europe in 1914, the IWW issued a resolution that declared, "We as members of the industrial army will refuse to fight for any purpose except the realization of industrial freedom." Two years later, the IWW General Executive Board issued a more pointed statement: "We will resent with all of the power at our command any attempt to compel us—the disinherited—to participate in a war that can only bring in its wake death and untold misery, privation, and suffering to millions of workers, and only serve to further rivet the chains of slavery on our necks, and render still more secure the power of the few to control the destinies of the many." To the Wobblies, the war was nothing more than a capitalist scheme to carve up international markets, a struggle that set worker against worker for the enrichment of industrialists selling goods to the warring powers.

On April 2, 1917, the same day that President Wilson stood before Congress to ask that war be declared against Germany, a convention of IWW delegates from Minnesota, Wisconsin, and Michigan released an announcement stating that in the event war was declared, the convention had voted approval of a resolution calling for a general industrial strike. The IWW declaration was carried in newspapers across the country. At a time when any expression of pacifism was considered "pro-German," and anything less than 100 percent support of the president was labeled "disloyalty," the IWW announcement was considered nothing less than treason.

Following America's entry into the conflict, the IWW's open opposition to the war, its call for strikes in industries critical to the war effort, and widespread reports of IWW sabotage of critical war commodities would put the organization on a collision course with the US Department of Justice and its auxiliary, the American Protective League.

Almost from its inception the League had been investigating the activities of the Industrial Workers of the World. With APL members at virtually every level of every industry throughout the United States, maintaining watch over the IWW had not proven difficult. As Charles Daniel Frey noted in his November 1918 "Report and Summary" of League activities prepared for the War Department's Military Intelligence Division:

> Because of the fact that the members of the League continue to follow their daily vocations and maintain their normal connections with the community, they are afforded unusual opportunities for the investigation of radical organizations of all kinds. The League has been able to introduce members into all of the more important organizations, and to report on their policies and activities, as well as upon the

activities of individual members. The number of investi-gations of this character carried on in the local (American Protective League) divisions were 3,645; or 25,515 for the entire country. As most of these were extended, and in many cases involved a complete report upon the local organization as a whole, the figures represent a very considerable amount of work. Under this heading are included investigations of the IWW.

The APL assigned operatives to infiltrate IWW locals, shadow IWW suspects, intercept the mail of individual Wobblies, and monitor IWW attendance at anti-war meetings—at times, dis-rupting them.

During his early days developing the Chicago Division, one of Frey's first recruits was 30-year-old Thomas Russell Gowenlock, a fellow Chicago adman that he appointed a Bureau Chief. A graduate of the University of Kansas Law School, Gowenlock had passed the bar but declined the legal field in favor of a busi-ness career, obtaining a position with the Gundlach Advertising Company of Chicago and later with H.W. Kastor & Sons Advertising Co., located in Chicago's Lytton Building. Like most Americans, after war had been declared Gowenlock was uncer-tain whether the United States would actually send an army to France or just support the Allied cause financially and materially. Taking temporary residence at the Chicago Beach Hotel and concerned that he wouldn't get beyond an army training camp if he immediately enlisted, Gowenlock accepted Frey's invita-tion to join the American Protective League until the part that America would play in the war became clear.

Similar to other businessman volunteers, Gowenlock viewed the League as a ready means for playing a valuable role in the war effort right in his own home town. By the late spring of 1917, he was a senior officer of the Chicago Division, heavily engaged in investigating radical organizations including the IWW. The young adman had been drawn to the APL's colors after read-ing about the impact that systematic German sabotage had been having on the supply of munitions to the Allied Powers during the years of American neutrality, and his recognition of the value that a domestic secret service organization would have in preventing such activity.

To Gowenlock, a natural extension of the struggle against enemy sabotage and subversion was the need to silence and disrupt "radical agitators"—German agents, anarchists, Bolsheviks, and the IWW, who appeared fixated on spreading "propaganda" in opposition to American participation in the war. Gowenlock believed that the oratory of IWW leaders and other radicals at mass meetings posed a grave threat to the country due to its potential for influencing indifferent and apathetic members of the general public to actively oppose the war.

"I was made a 'bureau chief' with a 'flying squad' of thirty men," Gowenlock later recalled. "Fifteen of these men were assigned from the Detective Bureau by its chief, Herman Schuettler, who picked them especially for the work." His squad included some of the toughest members of the Chicago Police force, seasoned veterans like Detectives McDonough and Egan of the Bomb Squad. The remaining members of Gowenlock's thirty-man company came from the APL volunteers who were now streaming into the organization from all quarters. With his hand-picked team of operatives, Gowenlock went into action, using information provided by the Justice Department and APL Division Headquarters to investigate and conduct daily raids on radical groups throughout greater Chicago.

At this time he was also handed a choice assignment: maintain surveillance on a fellow resident of the Chicago Beach Hotel, the infamous German secret service agent Gaston B. Means. Gaston Bullock Means was an operative of the Burns Detective Agency who had undertaken various missions for Germany during the spring and summer of 1915. As "Agent E-13" working for Naval Attaché Karl Boy-Ed, Means had carried out German propaganda assignments and arranged for supplies of critical commodities like rubber and copper to reach Germany by way of neutral European countries. But despite keeping Agent E-13 under watch around the clock for weeks on end, Gowenlock observed nothing out of the ordinary, for by now Means had abandoned clandestine work for the Germans in favor of a more profitable past-time: professional con man. (In July 1917, Gaston Means checked out of the Chicago Beach Hotel in the company of a wealthy widow, Maude King, who died a few months later of an "accidental" gunshot wound while on an outing with the notorious swindler.*)

Meanwhile Gowenlock's flying squad continued their campaign against radical opponents of the war, including those of the IWW. By day and night his men stealthily maneuvered into their secret mass meetings to seize the organizers and anyone else who spoke out openly against American participation in the European war. When the moment to apprehend the speakers came, a melee often ensued, with Gowenlock's squad literally fighting their way to an exit through a sea of radicals, their captives in tow.

On one occasion, Gowenlock and three of his Police Detective operatives slipped into an auditorium packed with over 500 anarchists who had gathered to protest US entry in the war as a scheme by American banking houses to protect their foreign investments. According to Gowenlock, "One of the orators began to damn the president, the government, and the flag. We grabbed the speaker. In a few seconds there were a thousand fists reaching for us." A riot call was placed to police headquarters and a score of officers appeared just in time to save them from being torn to pieces by the angry crowd.

Gowenlock also participated in America's first war riot. On May 27, 1917, a public forum was held at Chicago's Auditorium Theater to debate the peace terms that the Allies should demand of Germany and Austria-Hungary when the war ended. An overflow crowd resulted in thousands of people being denied entry to the event, and a huge throng proceeded to nearby Grant

---

* See Edwin P. Hoyt, *Spectacular Rogue: Gaston B. Means* (Indianapolis: Bobbs-Merrill Company, Inc., 1963), pp. 35–75.

Park where they were addressed by volunteer speakers at the bandshell. A well-known Socialist took the stage and announced "We demand that no men and no money be sent to Europe. We demand less power to the capitalists."

Sensing the mood of the crowd and anticipating trouble, police officers on the scene put in a call for reserves, and within minutes 300 to 400 Chicago policemen converged on the park together with a contingent of men from the American Protective League.

On the stage, the Socialist speaker concluded his speech. "I will now introduce to you someone who will talk to you from the viewpoint of the Russian workman." A bearded man with hat and walking stick strode out onto the stage. "This is a war of capital," he began. "The workmen are the sufferers. Why should American workmen fight the workmen of Germany for—?" Then followed an insult to President Wilson that, according to a *Chicago Tribune* reporter in attendance, "caused many to wince." In an instant there was trouble as enraged audience members moved onto the stage, and fighting quickly ensued. Policemen waded into the fray swinging riot batons to disperse the crowd. Gowenlock and three of his men made their way to the podium and grabbed one of the orators. "A few seconds later I landed on the heads of the people in front," Gowenlock later recounted. "My two companions rushed to me and, shoulder to shoulder, we battled for our lives. (If a riot call had not been put in) the results might have been disastrous—to us."

The *Chicago Tribune* reported: "As an easy yell of 'to hell with the government' rose out of the surging throng a quick moving secret service (APL) man or detective reached in and plucked for the offended. Before he could utter another peep he was thrust into a patrol wagon or taxicab and whisked away. Twenty or more secret service agents under the command of Captain T. B. Crockett (at that time the Assistant General Superintendent of the League) flitted here and there and silently garnered in the black sheep as they endeavored to stir the others to more violent resistance." Those arrested were taken to cells at local Chicago police stations or at the Federal Building.

Although politically and philosophically opposed to the war, the leadership of the Industrial Workers of the World also likely viewed it as an opportunity to extract higher wages and better working conditions for its members. As Vincent St. John had said, "Strikes are used when the employers can least afford a cessation of work . . . during the busy season and when there are rush orders to be filled . . ." With the war now on, industrialists struggling to meet delivery dates to satisfy the terms of government contracts for war materials could ill afford having their plants idled by a labor strike. During the spring and summer of 1917, IWW locals throughout the West and Midwest called for strikes in industries vital to the war effort. Timber strikes against loggers and sawmills soon broke out in the states of Oregon, Washington, and Idaho. IWW strikes were called against copper mines and smelters in Arizona and Montana. IWW dogma called for Wobblies in each branch of industry to help the other in gaining employer concessions. Rodger Culver, an IWW spokesman, declared, "If necessary to support the miner's demands, there will be no wheat crop in the North American continent [this season]."

An organized plot by labor insurgents to undermine the United States war effort appeared to be underway, thoroughly alarming politicians, the public, and the press. In July 1917, in the largest single government appropriation up to that time, a request for $640 million to build an air armada of 20,000 military aircraft had been submitted to Congress. The program would consume tremendous amounts of spruce from the Northwest and would be in peril without a reliable source of timber. War contracts had also been placed for huge quantities of artillery and small arms ammunition that in turn would require prodigious amounts of brass for the cartridge cases. Brass is a composition of copper and zinc, and the chief source of both during the war was the mines of the Southwest. Butte,

Montana alone, the site of major IWW strike activity, produced fifty percent of the zinc and twenty percent of the copper for the entire country. Without a reliable supply of copper and zinc, there would be no war.

Newspaper columns were soon filled with stories of alleged IWW chicanery and sabotage. Lumber mill saws were reportedly being destroyed by logs that IWW members had sabotaged with steel spikes. In orchard districts, fruit trees were dying because Wobblies had hammered copper nails into them. In Idaho, the IWW was reported to be importing phosphorus that would be placed in water containers in grain fields and around buildings where cereal was stored. When the water evaporated, the phosphorus would become combustible and burn the grain. Assertions from prominent individuals were also being published that German money was financing the IWW's activities, although the rumors to that effect were never proven.

The government initially believed that policing of IWW activities should be handled by state, rather than federal, authorities. However, by the summer of 1917 the IWW's actions, when taken in light of the past history of the organization, were such that an official Department of Justice investigation was begun. On July 17, 1917, Bureau of Investigation Chief Bielaski issued a letter to all special agents as well as APL investigative units:

> I enclose herewith for your information and immediate attention a copy of a letter which is being sent to the United States Attorney for your District, with respect to further investigation of the Industrial Workers of the World. This organization is apparently taking advantage of the needs of the country occasioned by the war to advance its own interests utterly without regard for the welfare of the people as a whole. It is desired that special efforts be made to the end that we may have the most complete information possible concerning the plans, organization, finances, leaders of the I.W.W., etc., and that as vigorous action as the law and the facts justify should be taken in every case.

An attached letter from the attorney general stated:

The Department has for some time past had under observation the activities of the Industrial Workers of the World
because of the announced intention of some of their members to interfere with the production, manufacture, and
transportation of food, munitions of war and other kinds of
supplies intended for use by the Government in the course
of the war with Germany. The announced principles of the
I.W.W., such as "direct action" and "sabotage", suggest opposition to the orderly conduct of governments. The present
war furnishes it with unusual opportunities for calling its
members into action against the interests of the people as a
whole and offers a situation which can readily be taken advantage of by agents of the German Government . . . While the
Department has been receiving much information concerning the situation, it desires that special efforts shall be made to
ascertain all of the plans of the members of this organization,
the names, description and history of its leaders, its sources of
income, the character of its expenses, copies of all literature
issued by it and all other data which may be useful to the
Department in determining what action may be taken under
the various criminal statutes of the United States.

Hinton G. Clabaugh, the Bureau of Investigation official to
whom Briggs had originally proposed his plan for an organization of citizen volunteers, was placed in charge of the IWW
investigation in Chicago. Clabaugh established a branch Bureau
of Investigation office in the McCormick Building. Manned by
a team of special agents supported by the American Protective
League members, the unit investigated the activities of the IWW
with a vengeance, obtaining key evidence of IWW violations of
the country's new Espionage Act.

The Espionage Act had been enacted into law by Congress
on June 15, 1917, as a reaction to the widespread fear of ongoing espionage by German agents and the inability of the government to deter it under existing federal laws. The Espionage

Act made it a crime to obtain, receive, or misuse information related to the national defense to injure the United States (punishment: a fine of not more than $10,000 or imprisonment for not more than two years, or both); to transfer national defense information that could be used to injure the United States to a foreign government, or a faction or party within a foreign country (punishment in time of war: death or imprisonment for not more than thirty years); during time of war, to willfully make or convey false statements with intent to interfere with the operation or success of US forces, promote the success of its enemies, or willfully cause or attempt to cause insubordination, disloyalty, mutiny, or refusal of duty in the US military, or to willfully obstruct the recruiting efforts of the United States to the injury of the service or of the United States (punishment: a fine of not more than $10,000 or imprisonment for not more than twenty years, or both). Individuals involved in a group conspiracy to carry out any of these actions would each receive the punishment designated under the law.

By this time it was no longer a secret that the Justice Department was investigating the IWW—it had become front page news. In July, the *Washington Post* reported:

> Wholesale arrests of IWW leaders are expected soon as the result of investigations being made by the Department of Justice into recent activities of the organization. The arrests, if made, will be under the authority of the Espionage Act. . . . While the Department of Justice is said to have been probing various acts charged to the IWW, it became known yesterday that added impetus had been given the investigation by pressure on the department from the capitol. Several Western senators have declared their intention of pushing the investigation of the organization to the limit and in the event of present laws being inadequate, to introduce special legislation designed to completely eliminate the IWW . . .

On August 16, 1917, the same day that the Wobblies called for a general strike in Washington, Oregon, Idaho, and

Montana unless the group's latest demands for better wages and conditions were met, the Associated Press released a news bulletin under the headline, "Drastic Treatment For IWW Threat":

WASHINGTON D.C.—The Department of Justice it was stated today, is prepared to deal swiftly and severely with activities in the northwest and elsewhere of the Industrial Workers of the World, in so far as they relate to the stoppage or curtailment of production in industries whose continuation is deemed essential to the prosecution of the war. Any action, it was said, which would tend to retard the harvesting of crops, the production of spruce lumber essential for the construction of airplanes, or to curtail the production of minerals needed to carry on the war, will be met by prosecution, on charges of conspiracy against persons regarded as responsible for the institution of the movement. A large force of investigators (including American Protective League operatives) is in the field in California, New Mexico, Arizona, Washington, Oregon, Idaho, and Montana, checking up and reporting daily upon activities of IWW leaders. Many industries whose continuance is necessary to the prosecution of the war would be affected, it is thought, by the threatened general strike in the northwest. District Attorney's throughout the entire section have been instructed by the department to institute promptly proceedings against strike leaders where such proceedings can be prosecuted under the broad powers given the president by congress in the war resolution. Cessation of labor in the harvest fields, in spruce logging camps or at mines, it is thought, would come clearly under the list of subjects which could be dealt with by federal authorities. Department officials knew several days ago of the impending demands of the Industrial Workers of the World in Washington, Oregon, Idaho, and Montana. Full details of the demands were in the hands of the department more than 48 hours before they had been announced yesterday by James Rowan, district secretary of the IWW in Spokane.

This last intelligence was likely provided by the infiltration of the organization by League operatives.

Three weeks later the Justice Department acted. On September 5, 1917, under the direction of Attorney General Gregory, United States Marshals descended on the headquarters of forty-eight IWW locals across the country. IWW offices in Duluth, Denver, Los Angeles, Seattle, San Francisco, Milwaukee, Minneapolis, Cleveland, Pittsburgh, and Chicago, among others, were simultaneously raided at 2 p.m. by the marshals and federal agents who seized a mass of IWW documents, including books, checks, membership records, meeting minutes, and correspondence. In Chicago, the raid on the IWW headquarters on West Madison Street by federal agents and city police culminated in the arrest of the IWW's leader, William "Big Bill" Haywood. At the same time, other federal agents and police raided the headquarters of the Socialist Party on nearby West Madison and served its counsel with a warrant for additional documents. The Department of Justice announced that the seizures were carried out as the result of a grand jury investigation underway in Chicago and that federal grand juries in other cities would also be called upon to investigate the Industrial Workers of the World.

The evidence obtained during the federal raids and by American Protective League investigations led to 165 IWW leaders being indicted by the Chicago grand jury and charged with the violation of a number of federal statutes, including conspiracy to prevent and hinder the government from executing the prosecution of the war; conspiracy to interfere with the production and transportation of food, clothing, and munitions essential to carrying on the war; conspiracy to interfere with the enforcement of the Selective Service Act; and conspiracy to violate the Espionage Act and to obstruct army and navy recruiting.

The trial of the IWW leadership took place in a courtroom at the Federal Building in Chicago and lasted for 128 days. At the time, it was the longest criminal trial in the country's history. The lead prosecutor was assisted by attorneys from the Justice Department, as well as by fifteen American Protective League lawyers who volunteered their time to assist the Bureau of Investigation to brief the evidence. The jury arrived at its verdict in sixty-five minutes, and the defendants were found guilty as charged by the indictment. Fifteen IWW members (including Haywood) each received a sentence of twenty years, thirty-five members received a sentence of ten years, thirty-three received a sentence of five years, and twelve Wobblies received a sentence of one year and a day. The remaining defendants were given lesser sentences. The IWW organization as a whole received fines that totaled $2,735,000. The case was later appealed all the way to the US Supreme Court, which upheld the verdict after which ten of the defendants skipped bail, including their leader, "Big Bill" Haywood, who fled to Soviet Russia, where he died a disillusioned man eight years later.

The "Great IWW Trial" in Chicago had a devastating impact on the Industrial Workers of the World movement. Subsequent IWW trials in Sacramento and Wichita during 1918 would further weaken the Wobblies. Never again would the "One Big Union" attain the 100,000-member mark that it held before the Great IWW Trial. Although many would later question whether the government's motivation in carrying out the September raids was to safeguard national defense efforts or eliminate a troublesome labor group, the American Protective League had helped to achieve what was seen in 1917 as a major victory in support of the Justice Department's "war at home." But it would not be the last time that the APL would cross paths with the IWW . . .

Now the League's efforts would be directed toward another obstacle confronting the American war effort, a vexing problem that was eliminating more soldiers from the US Army than enemy action: "the slackers."

CHAPTER 5

MOUNTING THE SLACKER RAIDS

It was chilly in Minneapolis on the night of March 26, 1918. Overhead, a full moon illuminated a clear black sky, and the city was quiet as the grave. This was particularly true in the Gateway lodging house district. The Gateway, a gritty skid row of cheap hotels and rooming houses, housed thousands of unskilled transient laborers who worked the Twin Cities' lumber mills and meatpackers or harvested outlying farms. They were the type of establishments where few questions were asked and where a man could lose himself if that's what he was trying to do.

By 11 p.m., after most residents had retired to their sleeping quarters for the night, a small convoy of trucks rumbled across the streets of the district and ground to a stop. One hundred and twenty American Protective League operatives swiftly dispersed from the trucks, accompanied by sixty-five Minnesota National Guardsmen armed with long Spanish-American War vintage Krag rifles, the hobnails of their heavy cowhide trench boots clattering on the pavement with every step.

Precisely to plan, the National Guardsmen assumed positions at the entrance and exit of each hotel, while units of League operatives, bright silver APL badges pinned to the outside of their coats glimmering in the moonlight, moved inside and began the hunt. Marching down the hotel corridors with determination, pounding on each door as they went, the Leaguers announced their arrival: "Open up, here to enforce the regulations of the United States Selective Service Act" and demanded that the residents come out of their rooms and produce their draft registration and certification cards. The bleary-eyed, disheveled laborers that answered the door invariably responded that they did indeed have draft cards. Each received the same response from the APL men, now being repeated throughout the district: "Show me . . ."

The Minneapolis APL operatives had been formally deputized as special officers of the Minnesota Public Safety Commission and had the legal authority to arrest and detain suspects. After an hour had passed, approximately 100 transients who could not produce the draft cards they were required to carry by law, were taken to a location that had been secured by the APL for temporary detention. There, Minneapolis APL Chief Davis and T. E. Campbell, a Bureau of Investigation agent, questioned the detainees regarding their draft status alongside several Assistant Chiefs and headquarters operatives. The interrogations continued until two in the morning, when most of the men were released on their own recognizance and instructed to report back later with proper credentials. Twenty-one others, identified as either army deserters, unregistered enemy aliens, or men whose draft status could not be satisfactorily determined, were marched off in the custody of the Minnesota National Guardsman to the county jail. The American Protective League officers and National Guard officers shook hands and congratulated each other on a good night's work, then turned out the light.

The first "slacker raid" in the nation had officially been carried out.

"You slacker!" Today the expression is typically used as a jibe to suggest that someone is avoiding work, lazy, or not performing at 100 percent. But during World War I the expression had a very different meaning—"slacker" meant "draft dodger," and during that period of intense patriotism and nationalistic pride, "slacker" was a serious, even dangerous, accusation.

The manpower requirements necessary to field an army capable of turning the tide in Europe had eliminated the possibility of raising an army of volunteers, so on May 18, 1917, Woodrow Wilson signed the Selective Service Act into law. The new draft system would be unlike any previous draft in American history—it would be truly compulsory and it would be truly comprehensive. Under the conscription regulations introduced during the Civil War, a draftee could hire a substitute soldier to stand in his place or pay a $300 charge to "buy" a draft exemption, but during World War I things would be different. On the same day that Wilson signed the new draft legislation, he fixed June 5, 1917, as the date when 10.2 million American men between the ages of twenty-one and thirty-one would be required to register for military service. An army of 500,000 would be immediately selected from that number for training. Those subject to the draft registration were required to register at the local voting place in their city or town, and those that failed to register on June 5 would be subject to arrest and imprisonment for one year. Any man who expected to be absent from his home precinct on the registration date could appear before his city clerk to complete a registration card in advance. If a man was confined to his home or a hospital by illness, he was to make arrangements to have a representative apply to the clerk for a registration card, who would also receive instructions on how to complete it.

Under the 1917 draft regulations, few men would be exempt from military service. The only exceptions were men indispensable to military industries; men with wives, children, parents, or siblings that depended solely upon them for support; members of well-recognized religious sects whose creeds forbid them to bear arms, such as the Quakers or Amish; legislative, judicial, and executive officers of the United States; subjects of Germany; workmen in US armories and arsenals; men engaged in the transmission of US mail; members of the United States Merchant Marine; and criminals that had been convicted of felonies. Every other male within the age range was subject to registration.

As the date of the first draft registration drew near, no one was sure whether it would be a success or a failure, since nothing like it had been tried on a similar scale before. Within a fourteen-hour period, 11 percent of the country's population was expected to register, and there was certain to be disorder and confusion at the polling places where the draft registration would take place. In addition to native born Americans, men from a wide range of ethnic and cultural groups speaking a multitude of languages were expected to appear; in New York City alone, fifty-two foreign languages were being spoken at the time. To help bring order to the anticipated confusion, Attorney General Gregory requested that the American Protective League render assistance.

Shortly before 7 a.m. on June 5, "Registration Day," 80,000 APL members appeared at voting places throughout the country to give advice to the registrants and render assistance to the draft officials. On the day of the first registration, their help was sorely needed. As described in the League's authorized history, "In the larger cities, particularly those with large foreign born populations, great congestion resulted because of ignorance of the law and its provisions on the part of registrants, and because of the difficulty in ascertaining and correctly transcribing their names and other information regarding them. The number of places for registration proved insufficient because of the shortness of the hours, and in many places great confusion resulted. Acting under proper instructions, members of the League in large numbers served as volunteer registrants under the direction of the officials." The League would turn out again for the second great draft registration on September 12, 1918, when more than 200,000 members were sent to the registration polls to render assistance.

The first registration proved to be a great success, with more men inducted than the army had material and equipment with which to supply and train them. Although registering for the draft was widely accepted as a civic duty and a necessity to protect the nation during its time of peril, across the country there was scattered opposition to the draft from the start. The day before the first registration was held, nine men were arrested in Pennsylvania and charged with treason for distributing anticonscription literature. Indictments charging conspiracy to interfere with the registration were filed against seven individuals in New York. A man in Boston was arrested for advising two young men of draft age not to register. In Minneapolis, a Socialist was arrested for distributing handbills containing anticonscription resolutions made by the National Socialist convention. In Montana, a company of infantry from the Second Montana Regiment was even dispatched to Butte due to the appearance of anticonscription pamphlets in various parts of the city. The ineffective street corner oratory of the arrested draft opponents proved to be a problem easily dealt with, but a genuine cause of concern to government authorities was the fact that although nearly 10 million men had registered for the draft, over 200,000 "slackers" had not registered—enough potential recruits to create an army in itself.

The large number of nonregistrants was due at least in part to the fact that evading capture as a draft dodger was not particularly difficult during World War I. Although the daily newspapers carried stories about men skipping the country for Mexico or Canada to sit out the war—and what would happen to them when they returned—the typical draft evader remained in the United States since few means existed for law enforcement to track them down. In a time without Social Security numbers, credit cards, online credit reporting services, or cell phones, all that a "slacker" had to do to avoid capture by the authorities was stay mobile. Most of the wartime draft dodgers and "deserters" (men who had registered for the draft and then disappeared) remained constantly on the move, roaming from town to town under assumed names, often not staying in any one location more than a week.

Viewed as scoundrels that had deserted their country during its struggle for existence, slackers and deserters could expect no sympathy or assistance from the population at large. Draft evaders were vilified in the press and the subject of scorn and derision in the new medium of motion pictures. A popular 1917 film that was aptly titled, "The Slacker," told the story of two young children, Bobby and Daisy, who enlist in the army as a soldier and nurse because "We didn't want to be slackers." At one point in the film, an army officer turns to a crowd of draft-age men and asks, "Will you let these babies put you to shame?" Once identified as a slacker, the best that a draft evader could hope for would be getting run out of town. More typically they were handed over to the draft authorities for immediate induction into the army—or sent to prison, if they refused.

The most infamous slacker, the "best hated man in America," was Grover Cleveland Bergdoll. The wealthy son of a Philadelphia brewer (his grandfather had founded the successful Bergdoll Brewing Company), Bergdoll was a well-known playboy sportsman who owned several fast automobiles that he raced with his brother Erwin, along with several aircraft that he personally flew. As a German-American, Bergdoll had strong sympathies with the Fatherland when the war began, and early in 1914 offered his services to Germany as an aviator through the local German consul. After the United States became involved in the war, Bergdoll announced that he would never fight against Germany. He ignored a draft call and disappeared in August 1917. Due to his notoriety, an extensive search was made for Bergdoll throughout the United States, Mexico, and Cuba. He was alleged to have been seen at various times in Mexico, on a Western United States ranch, in Spain, in western New York, or at home in Philadelphia. Several times authorities searched the Bergdoll family's three palatial estates in Philadelphia without success. Meanwhile, as Bergdoll moved from one location to another to evade capture, he tantalized the public with postcards sent to newspapers and taunted his infuriated draft board with cards mailed from towns and cities around the country. As the war progressed, newspapers continued to ask, "Where is Grover Cleveland Bergdoll?"

Bergdoll's continued liberty underscored the fact that tracking down an individual slacker or deserter was a very difficult task for the government. As early as August 1917, the League joined government authorities to track down draft evaders. In a general bulletin distributed on August 4, Assistant Superintendent T. B. Crockett notified all chiefs that:

> The Federal Government is conducting a thorough and country-wide investigation for the detection and prosecution of all male persons within the required ages who did not register under the conscription act for the selective draft. The United States Department of Justice, Bureau of Investigation has instructed the American Protective League to take up this work in each and every district. It is of vital importance to the government that those who have escaped detection and prosecution under the conscription act be apprehended, registered and prosecuted. To that end the Department of Justice desires a prompt and thorough search for these persons followed by rigorous criminal prosecution of all those apprehended.

On February 6, 1918, Provost Marshal General Enoch Crowder and Attorney General Gregory united in a request sent to the American Protective League to "cooperate with all local and district exemption boards in locating and assisting to present themselves to the proper authorities those now classified as 'delinquents' (slackers) or deserters under the Selective Service regulations."

In a letter sent to the governors of all the states, Provost Marshal General Crowder requested that "every Local [Draft] Board is to have at least one of the agents of the American Protective League attached to it, and, in the larger cities, it is expected that several will be attached to each Local Board, the number depending upon the registrants under the jurisdiction of the Board. Will you please urge each Local Board in your state to utilize the services of this organization to the fullest extent. If this is done, there is no doubt that the results will be highly satisfactory and that an invaluable aid will be rendered by these patriotic citizens during this emergency."

Although APL divisions received lists of wanted draft evaders from local and district draft boards, due to confusion in the spelling of names, inaccurate records, and the transient roaming nature of much of the nation's blue collar work force, actually bringing them in was another matter. The effort required to catch a single slacker—who often as not had just innocently forgotten to report a change of address or draft status to his local board— could consume the time of several APL operatives for weeks.

And finding the draft evaders had become critical to the war effort. General Pershing notified the War Department that due to the situation the Allies were facing in France (Bolshevik Russia left the war in 1918, freeing up huge reserves of German soldiers for the Western Front) he would require several times the number of soldiers that he now had at his command. This in turn would result in additional draft registrations across a broader age range, but these new registrations would not yield many of the most suitable twenty-one- to thirty-one-year-olds who had already been called up and accounted for in the first registration—except for the missing slackers and deserters. Orders went out from the Department of Justice to mobilize the entire American Protective League to "throw out the net for slackers."

The results of the first slacker raid in Minnesota's Gateway lodging house district had proven that "raiding" was the most efficient and effective approach for capturing slackers. Instead of the time-intensive pursuit of a single individual roaming from town to town, the League would form an inescapable cordon around a likely area for potential draft evaders and then sort through the catch for "genuine" slackers, thereby ensuring the best results with the least amount of time and effort. Convinced that there could be hundreds of other men in Minneapolis ignoring the draft regulations, the Minneapolis APL Division decided to follow up the Gateway incursion with a citywide slacker raid.

On the evening of April 6, 1918, 250 American Protective League operatives accompanied by 700 Minnesota National

Guardsmen set out on patrol throughout the city in search of slackers. From 8 p.m. to 10 p.m., the League members and their National Guard escorts visited 197 pool rooms, cafes, dance halls, and saloons, taking into custody any man of draft age not carrying his draft registration credentials. Within that two-hour span, over 1,150 men were picked up, loaded into moving vans and motor trucks, and taken to temporary detention quarters set up in the assembly room of the city's courthouse. There the APL chief and a corps of assistants interrogated the detainees, only releasing them after proof of satisfactory draft status had been ascertained.

"My draft classification card is at home, can't I go after it?" was the typical response from potential draft evaders being held in detention. "Have it brought here. We have to see it. Use the telephone . . ." was the standard reply from the APL officers questioning them. As a result, the local and long-distance telephone and telegraph wires from the courthouse were kept busy throughout the night. A process of elimination ensued until the following day when only twenty-seven individuals remained, who were sent to the county jail for violation of the Selective Service Act regulations.

According to the "Summary and Report of War Service," published by the Minneapolis Division of the League after the war:

> As a result of the activities of the American Protective League in Minneapolis, there were finally inducted into the military service, either as delinquents or as draft deserters, a total of 1,261. These men were not all local men; in fact, a large portion of them were men from other cities. Hundreds of these were men who had registered for the draft, June 5, 1917, and immediately left the city where they were registered, with the avowed intention of evading the draft by moving from place to place, and scores of them admitted upon their arrest that they had not stayed in one place at any time to exceed one week. Thus the Minneapolis Division was represented in uniform by two and one-half times its total membership by those who would not otherwise have seen service. The zeal with which our operatives followed up a case of this sort is partially

explained when you realize what a large percentage of them had tried to get into the military service themselves and had been turned down for some minor defect.

Across the country, other American Protective League divisions mounted similar raids in pursuit of draft evaders during the summer of 1918. League operatives in Columbus, Ohio, spent several nights raiding saloons, wine rooms, and pool halls in an effort to locate some of that state's estimated 20,000 slackers. One thousand men were rounded up in Des Moines, Iowa. A series of raids by deputy marshals and American Protective League operatives throughout the wards in New Orleans resulted in 250 men without draft cards taken into custody, 100 of whom were eventually charged. Two thousand suspected slackers were taken into custody in a Davenport, Iowa, raid by 500 city and federal agents. In Cleveland, 300 APL operatives took 1,000 men without draft cards before the district draft examining board. Six hundred men were apprehended on Atlantic City's four pleasure piers, yielding 60 "genuine" slackers. Another slacker drive in Milwaukee, Wisconsin, netted so many draft-age men without proper credentials that each suspect was released on a $500 bond until he could prove his draft status, purely to avoid an overflow at the local jails.

The American Protective League even joined in the hunt for Grover Cleveland Bergdoll, America's most infamous slacker. In July 1918, eleven months after he began his life on the run, the draft evader sent a letter to the *Public Ledger* to announce that if the army made him a flight instructor he would reappear to join the nation's colors. He also claimed that he had enough money to keep him and his motor car running for ten years. After reading Bergdoll's letter, Philadelphia District Attorney Francis Fisher Kane sought the League's assistance in capturing Bergdoll, and provided several tantalizing clues to his present location. Bergdoll's letter had been posted at a station on the Erie Railroad between Jersey City and Salamanca, in Western New York. He was believed to have then traveled to Buffalo, or perhaps Chicago.

In a front page article published in the League's official bulletin, *The Spy Glass*, under the headline, "Draft Dodger Bergdoll Wanted by U.S.A.," the organization alerted all members to be on the watch for him. "Bergdoll has a fancy for dark brown clothes and shoes of the same color . . . His taste in ties runs to loud colors . . . Being a motor fan, it is safe to assume that wherever he is, part of his time will be spent in a car. Help to show him—and other slackers like him—that money can't buy exemption from the duties of citizenship." The article included a prewar photograph of a smirking Grover Cleveland Bergdoll. Despite the 250,000 League operatives on the lookout from coast to coast for "the best hated man in America," Bergdoll's whereabouts remained a mystery.

Meanwhile, the most spectacular slacker drive to occur that summer took place between July 11 and 14 in Chicago. The Chicago APL division was the largest and best-organized division in the League, and its drive was bold, well-planned, and all encompassing. The entire Chicago League membership was mobilized for the effort—over 10,000 operatives in all. No announcements were made.

In the early hours of July 11, squads of Chicago APL operatives began to move simultaneously throughout the city in search of draft evaders. All of the city's ball parks were visited, the crowds being told to file out of designated gates, at which point every draft-age male had to show his registration card or face detention. Movie theatres were handled the same way. Operatives appeared at the Lake Michigan beaches in swimsuits, wading out to question bathers in the water; over 100 draft evaders were captured "in the wet." At night, cabarets and night clubs were canvassed, and the city parks were patrolled in search of slackers and deserters. At a major boulevard that crossed the Chicago Loop district, every automobile was stopped and its driver and passengers examined. During the four days of the drive, APL operatives questioned the occupants of every incoming train, theatre, public building, "L" road station, steamboat landing, factory, store, saloon, and pedestrian thoroughfare. Even Sunday picnics were inspected. The courts and jails were soon crammed with detainees, as was the Federal Building. Vacant store-rooms overflowed with prisoners. When the drive had been completed, 200,000 draft-age men had been questioned and over 20,000 taken into custody. Of these, 1,400 men were inducted into the army—enough soldiers for a battalion of infantry.

Despite the sweeping scope of the Chicago drive and the number of individuals questioned, detained, or taken into temporary custody, there was no public criticism. The reaction of Chicago's populace to the city-wide slacker drive is best described by the following editorial that appeared at the time in the *Chicago Tribune:*

> Americans do not like to be interfered with by officials. They are not accustomed to it, and they resent it in normal times, even when it is quite justifiable. But though it has been by no means convenient to be stopped on the way to work, interrogated, sent back home for credentials or taken in custody pending investigation, there has been in this roundup a general good-natured acceptance of the process, and in the vast majority of cases, a cordial co-operation with the authorities.
>
> A part of the credit for this undoubtedly belongs to the tact and good sense shown by the draft authorities and the volunteers of the American Protective League, who deserve congratulation upon the skill with which they have accomplished a by no means easy task with a minimum of friction and a maximum of thoroughness. But if the authorities showed good spirit, the public met them half way, and the total experience proves the excellent morale now existing. Whatever is necessary to get on with the war is accepted without complaint. Virtually everybody wants to help. Furthermore, the number of slackers found in proportion to the number of men questioned is gratifyingly small.

As the summer of 1918 drew to a close, the army remained in urgent need of additional manpower. Following the great German spring offensive, the Allies had called on the US government to establish an army of 120 divisions of 40,000 soldiers each in Europe (4.8 million men) and to maintain a further reserve of 1 million men at home. The War Department responded with a plan calling for 80 divisions (3.2 million men) in Europe and 720,000 men in reserve at home. Even after expanding the age range for draft eligibility (decreasing the minimum age from twenty-one to eighteen and increasing the maximum age from thirty-one to forty-five), based on the number of exempt, physically unfit, or otherwise disqualified registrants anticipated in future registrations, more men would still be needed.

On August 15, Secretary of War Newton Baker sent a letter to Attorney General Gregory, stating that, "The record of desertion under the first and second drafts disclosed the fact that on June 10, 1918 there [has] existed a known desertion from both drafts of 308,489 men." If true, this amounted to the equivalent of approximately twenty-five divisions of potential soldiers. The army's provost marshal made renewed demands to the Justice Department to locate and make available for induction into the army the thousands of slackers and deserters still at large.

Ten days later, A. Bruce Bielaski, chief of the Bureau of Investigation, advised the National Directors of the American Protective League that he wanted a city-wide slacker drive, similar to the Chicago effort, to take place in New York City as soon as possible. Planning was soon under way for a sweeping search for draft evaders that would encompass not only New York City, but all of Westchester County and Jersey City, Newark, Hoboken, and Paterson, New Jersey. The drive would take place on September 3, 4, and 5, 1918.

The scope of this slacker campaign would dwarf even the Chicago drive conducted a few months earlier. The total number of federal agents, American Protective League members, special deputies, and police that would participate in the roundup would total between 20,000 and 25,000 men. This sizable force would be further augmented by 2,000 army soldiers and 1,000 sailors from posts in New York City. There would be at least one operative or agent to every block in the principal business and residential sections of the drive. To transport suspected draft evaders, a fleet of cars and trucks had been requisitioned—over 400 vehicles for Manhattan and a further 250 for Brooklyn. To hold individuals for questioning, four detention headquarters were established: for New York City and the Bronx, the Sixty-Ninth Regiment Armory; for Brooklyn, the Twenty-Third Regiment Armory; for Jersey City, the Fourth Regiment Armory; and for Newark, the First Regiment Armory.

Procedures for apprehending, transporting, and processing suspected draft evaders were carefully formulated. The instructions to the members of the mixed force participating in the drive were simple and direct: "Every man who, *judging from his appearance* [author's emphasis], had not reached his thirty-first birthday by June 5, 1917, or who up to August 24, 1918, had not attained the age of twenty-one, should be requested to show his draft registration certificate. Individuals with no registration and/or certificate are to be held [for investigation]."

After apprehending the suspect, the operative was to bring him to the nearest police station. As soon as possible thereafter, or whenever a police station had collected an automobile-load of detained suspects, they were to be transported to one of the established detention headquarters where an examining board of draft officials would then inquire into their case.

Each suspect would be given a yellow* card to fill out. According to the plan, if the man was registered, that fact would be quickly ascertained by a telephone call to his district draft board to verify the answers provided on the yellow card. If the board confirmed that the suspect had registered and was in compliance with the draft regulations, the yellow card would be exchanged for a white receipt, to serve as an honorable discharge from custody. If the board reported that he was not registered,

---

* Men who were suspected of draft evasion were given a yellow card, which must have seemed to some like they were being considered *yellow*—or a coward. Likely unintentional, but possibly unsettling to those who received one.

the detainee was to be transferred to the nearest police station and held there pending action from the federal government. If a suspect was from another part of the country and unable to produce proper draft credentials, he was to remain in custody until his status could be determined by telegraph.

Evaluated in the light of the recent successful operations in Chicago and around the country, the preparations for the New York slacker drive must have seemed adequate to those who would lead the effort. But closer examination should have given reason for pause. Except for Minnesota APL operatives who had been deputized and had the legal authority to arrest and detain suspects, no American Protective League operatives possessed the legal authority to arrest *anyone*. The APL was an investigative body only, expected to obtain evidence of violations of federal law to be delivered to duly authorized law enforcement officials. Even the special agents from the Bureau of Investigation had no power to arrest lawbreakers and would not obtain that right from Congress until 1935.

Another potential problem with the New York drive was the size of the operation itself. With over 20,000 individuals from private, city, state, federal, and military organizations involved in the roundup, it would be difficult to supervise the project once it was underway.

The factor of surprise, critical to the success of all previous slacker raids, was lost at the start of the 1918 New York drive. While thousands of APL operatives, policemen, federal agents, and military personnel were rushing to their assigned duty locations for the 7 a.m. launch on September 3, the morning edition of the *New York Times*, being delivered to doorsteps throughout the area, included the story titled, "Start Drive Today for Draft Slackers: Men Between 21 and 31 Will Be Stopped Today and Asked to Show Registration Cards," that included complete details of the operation: who was involved, who they were after, and where they would be operating. Subsequent updates on the slacker drive would be contained in editions of the newspaper published on September 4 through 6 that provided a running account of the preceding days' activities. The only draft evaders who would be captured in the New York and New Jersey raids would be those who didn't read local newspapers—or didn't know someone who did.

Despite the publicity, the raids continued as planned. The first suspected draft evaders were apprehended at the city railroad stations. By 6:30 a.m., the stations and ferry-houses of every railroad connected with New York City were being patrolled by APL operatives, and every arriving male passenger of draft age questioned. Within three and a half hours, between 2,000 and 2,500 of those arrivals were being held in the 69th Regiment Armory, the out-of-state detainees being sent to the east end of the building and New York natives herded into the "bullpen"—a roped space in the center of the armory floor.

Local residents immediately placed telephone calls to family members asking them to hurry to the armory with whatever cards they could find that had been issued to them by their local draft board. As a result, an hour later the armory was besieged by relatives and friends of the men inside. In time, the rush became so great that the visitors had to be driven from the armory into the street. The iron gates were closed, and 720 soldiers from the Mulberry Park barracks were stationed around the armory to deny entry. Meanwhile, the only thing that the out-of-town men could do was send a telegram to their distant homes requesting that their draft records be sent, then sit down, and wait . . .

All areas of New York City and northern New Jersey were now being patrolled in search of draft delinquents and deserters. Sailors and APL operatives formed a gauntlet at the doors of every theatre and called for registration cards from any man who appeared to be of draft age. In restaurants and hotels, League members moved from table to table asking for draft cards. The solicitations were made courteously, but those being questioned quickly came to the realization that the men from the League were not to be trifled with. As soon as a squad of ten or twelve suspects had been collected at any one point, they were marched off to the nearest police station. By midday, guards were posted at most city corners; each block was closed and diligently searched for draft evaders.

A large group of alleged slackers was rounded up on Fifth Avenue and Lafayette Place. A passing truck was commandeered, and the men were taken to the 69th Street armory. When they arrived, someone thought to question the driver of the truck, and it was discovered that in fact the driver himself did not have his draft credentials. He was promptly added to the group of detainees and his employer was notified to send someone to pick up the truck.

Confusion reigned at the armory buildings where the men were being held. One of the men seized, defense worker Perry Acker, was kept standing in line for four hours only to learn that he had been approved for discharge hours before but didn't know it. There were hundreds of similar cases. The roundup had proceeded at such a rapid pace during the first day that by nightfall the number of men seized exceeded the means to process them, and "slow down" orders had to be issued to those searching for draft evaders. By then, a staggering 32,000 suspects had been seized and taken to the various detention headquarters. It was estimated that between 10,000 and 12,000 men had been apprehended in Manhattan, 8,000 to 10,000 in Brooklyn, Queens, Coney Island, and Long Island, and another 2,200 in the Bronx. A further 12,000 men had been picked up in New Jersey.

The second day of the slacker drive saw a decided reduction in the number of men taken into custody, since most were now prepared to be stopped and asked for their draft cards. Still, over 1,000 men were arrested in the Bronx on street cars, at elevated and subway stations, and in theatres. A corral was established at 149th Street and Willis Avenue, where the prisoners were herded before taken to the Alexander Avenue police station. At the various armory detention headquarters, while many of the local men apprehended on the first day had been processed and sent on their way, the out-of-town detainees were by then in a bad way. In nearly every case they had been unable to get any reply from their local draft boards. Joseph Rubene, a butler from Lenox, Massachusetts, was taken into custody at Grand Central Station. Although Rubene had his registration card, he did not have his classification card. Rubene sent six telegrams to his draft board but received no reply and was still in captivity two days after being picked up. After just one day in captivity, Pierre Flotow of New Orleans had reached the point where he offered to pay his own fare to New Orleans, and that of a government guard to accompany him, to prove that he was not a slacker.

By the time the New York slacker raids ended, on the third and final day of the drive, an estimated 50,271 men had been taken into custody. Of those, 15,000 were turned over to their local draft boards as delinquents or to have their draft status corrected, 1,000 were inducted and sent directly to army camps, and 250 were held by order of the court. But by then, the slacker drive, and the way that it had been conducted, was being roundly condemned by the public and press alike.

An editorial published in the *New York Times* on September 6, 1918, titled "Slacker Hunt," gave a harsh appraisal of the New York roundup:

> As the draft slacker is held in unspeakable contempt, it must be very hard for a good citizen to be suspected of evading military service, to be looked upon by curious crowds as a craven or as an alien enemy; and yet that has been the experience of many thousands of duly registered men during the 'slacker drive' which the Federal authorities are conducting in this city with more zeal than judgment. The draft is popular, but it may be brought into disfavor by rough and ready enforcement of the law.
>
> The manner in which the 'slacker hunt' was planned and directed has no sensible man's approval. It ought not to have been necessary to fill armory and police station with hosts of registered men to run down a comparatively few draft dodgers. There were cases of real hardship. It isn't always easy to produce the proof that Federal agents in such cases demand.

Perhaps the safer way would be to carry a registration card until it is worn to a frazzle, but no one is inclined to do that . . .

The next time the Department of Justice orders a 'slacker hunt' for effect on new registration, it should be less spectacular and more practical. We have no doubt that the press-gang method adopted lost the authorities a good many recreants, who stayed under cover. Would not persistent detective work—the Justice Department has money enough—have netted more slackers than beating up the highways, theatres, and restaurants?

The New York drive even created a furor on the floor of the United States Senate. On the same day that the *New York Times* editorial was published, Utah Senator Reed Smoot introduced a resolution calling on the Senate Military Affairs Committee to investigate what happened in New York. Senator George Chamberlain of Oregon, chairman of the Military Affairs Committee, launched into a fiery denunciation of the Department of Justice, declaring that its methods in the slacker raids savored of "Prussianism." "If the department would devote more time to catching pro-Germans and spies it would not have so much time to round up whole communities of innocent persons as draft evaders," Chamberlain proclaimed. New York Senator William Calder followed by reading a letter into the Congressional Record from a citizen of New York, name withheld: "This man was dining in Brooklyn with a woman on the first night of the drive. Suddenly he was seized by the military police and taken to the Seventy-fourth Precinct police station, and from there to the Twenty-Third Regiment Armory, where he was kept standing with several hundred others from 10 p.m. until 5 a.m." Senator Thomas of Colorado interrupted Calder to say that, "assuming the contents of the letter to be true, I think the author of this drive ought to be dismissed from public service and I do not hesitate to say so." "Russia," said Senator Fall of New Mexico, "is the only place in the world where such actions could take place under civil rule." "There is no law to cover it," Senator Chamberlain interjected, "the fact is men are afraid in this wartime to assert their rights and stand up for their liberties. That's why so many innocent men were dragged off to jail. In other times, men would have resented arrest, and would have killed those who tried to seize them without authority of law."

In an effort to head off the growing scandal, President Wilson ordered Attorney General Gregory to investigate the New York slacker drive and to provide him with a report of his findings. In the report that followed, Gregory assumed full responsibility for granting approval for the New York slacker raids, but condemned the methods by which the New York drive had been carried out as unlawful and contrary to his instructions:

> In order to set forth intelligently the proceedings at New York it is necessary to touch on a serious national problem. There are many deserters and slackers at large in this country.
>
> The Secretary of War referred to this condition as 'an indictment against the honor of the nation.' To permit it to continue would weaken substantially the nation's fighting power and do grievous injustice to the great body of the youth of the land who so gallantly met their military obligations. Energetic measures were required. The Secretary of War naturally looked to this department for assistance. To attempt to apprehend so great a number of offenders by running down individual cases obviously would have been futile. Some form of dragnet process, within the law of course, was absolutely essential.
>
> It was accordingly decided to adopt the plan of canvassing, or rounding up in the large cities, on particular days all men apparently within the draft age and arranging for a summary and immediate investigation of their status through their local draft boards. Of necessity this involved detaining, pending investigation, all men who did not have registration or classification cards (which registrants are required by the regulations to keep always in their personal possession), or who were not able to establish by satisfactory evidence that they were outside the draft ages. It was expected that for the

most part such men would voluntarily go to the places of detention, which were usually armories, while the investigation of their status was being made. Where arrests were necessary it was never contemplated that they should be made by any but police officials of the United States, or of the States and municipalities where the canvass was being conducted. The making of arrests in such cases by the military, or by the members of any private organization, would have been contrary to law and contrary to the express directions of the Attorney General, except in the case of deserters, where, of course, the military authorities had the power to make arrests. It was expected, however, that where the number detained was large, this department in making the necessary investigation, would have the aid of the American Protective League, a private organization of established standing which had long been participating in the enforcement of the selective service law by express invitation of the Provost Marshal General; and that in guarding the persons taken into custody it would have the aid of units of the military and naval forces.

While this plan was evolved in discussion with a representative of the Provost Marshal General's office, I take full and entire responsibility for adopting it and for putting it into effect. I know that some such dragnet process is necessary unless thousands upon thousands of deserters and slackers are to remain at large; I believe the plan adopted is authorized by the regulations; I believe also, judging by the results at a number of different points, that the great body of our people will cheerfully submit to the minor inconveniences which the execution of any such plan of necessity entails, to the end that this indictment of the nation's honor, this drain on the nation's strength, may be removed. I shall, therefore, continue to employ the plan unless you give directions to the contrary.

Coming to the city of New York, I again accept full and entire responsibility for putting into effect there the general plan of rounding up deserters and slackers which I have described. Contrary to my express instructions, however, instructions which I have repeated over and over again, and contrary to law, certain members of the investigating force of this department, without consultation with me or with any law officer of the department, used soldiers and sailors and certain members of the American Protective League, I am satisfied, in making arrests. I am convinced by the inquiries which I have made that they were led into this breach of authority by excess of zeal for the public good. While this extenuates, it does not excuse their action.

When Wilson released the attorney general's report to the newspapers on September 12, 1918, the action appeared to signal the president's approval of the use of the "raid process" to capture draft evaders, and the excesses of the New York drive were soon forgotten. APL slacker raids and drives would continue in the few months that remained before the Armistice in Europe, including a major three-day drive in the state of Washington, which marked the first *statewide* raid in the nation. During these final operations, APL operatives would always be accompanied by authorized state and federal lawmen, who performed the actual arrests.

The American Protective League assisted in the apprehension of between 20,000 and 25,000 draft delinquents and deserters for induction into the US Army during World War I. At the time this was viewed as one of the organization's stellar achievements in assisting the government to prosecute the war. But the New York slacker drive, in which thousands of innocent men were indiscriminately arrested and detained, brought the League for the first time into disrepute, and focused national attention on the secret organization's operatives and their methods.

CHAPTER 6

OPERATIVES AND METHODS

The white schooner cast off just before sunrise. Gliding past Faro Lighthouse into Mazatlan Harbor, it joined in with a small fleet of tuna boats grouping in the darkness before heading off toward the rich fishing grounds of the Sea of Cortez. By day-break, the Mexican shoreline had become a thin sliver on the horizon as the white schooner abruptly veered away from the fishing boats and took a course toward the northwest. Unlike the fishermen now dropping their nets in the hope of landing a catch of dorado, wahoo, or tuna, the men on the schooner had a different quarry in mind—they intended to prey on the rich Allied shipping plying the peaceful waters of South America. For the *Agassiz* was no ordinary schooner, it was a German commerce raider embarking on its maiden voyage for the Fatherland.

Built in San Diego in 1907, the *Alexander Agassiz* was a forty-one-ton, sixty-one-foot long, two-masted auxiliary schooner, with twin screw engines. Following several years in the service of a biological institute located at La Jolla, California, the *Agassiz* had been sold to the Pacific Trading Company where she was used for a time to carry oysters from Tombari Bay in the Gulf of California to a floating cannery in Magdalena Bay. When the quality of the oyster harvest had declined to a level that made it financially nonviable, the *Agassiz* had been taken off that run and entered into service between Mazatlan and Manzanillo, Mexico. It was while sitting in drydock alongside the Mexican customs house at Mazatlan that the *Alexander Agassiz* had suddenly and discretely changed from American to Mexican registry.

On that day of March 22, 1918, the Agassiz was sailing under orders of the German Consul Unger at Mazatlan. On board were five German nationals, six Mexicans, and two American women—one the ship's fiery red-haired owner, Maude Lochrane. The schooner also carried a small arsenal of rifles, pistols, and ammunition, enough provisions for a three-month voyage, and for future use, an Imperial German Navy flag. The German plan was bold. They would first proceed to Vernados Island to pick up Fritz Bauman, who would serve as captain. Bauman was a former German naval reservist who for a time had been the chief officer of one of the German merchant ships interned at Santa Rosalia. They would next set sail for Santa Rosalia itself, where additional German deckhands would board while she was fitted with heavy machine guns and the advanced instruments necessary for long-range cruising. The *Alexander Agassiz* would then depart on her new career as a German raider preying on the western sea trade. The first victim was to be a Pacific mail boat running to Panama, likely followed by a succession of merchant freighters.

The passage to Vernados was progressing smoothly with the Germans in high spirits, when a cry rang out: "Ship approaching—port side . . ." All eyes turned to the west. There *was* a ship on the horizon . . . a big ship with black coal smoke pouring from a single funnel growing larger by the second as it bore down on them at terrific speed. The men aboard the *Agassiz* snapped into action. The schooner turned sharply and made a dash for the open sea at full power.

The ship following in fast pursuit was the *USS Vicksburg*, a 1,010-ton Annapolis class gunboat that had been on the alert for the incipient German raider since receiving a warning message by wireless from Naval Command several days before. Commissioned in 1897, the *Vicksburg* was equipped with a single screw engine and a full barkentine rig of sails for extended cruising. It was formidably armed with a brace of four-inch, six-pounder, and one-pounder cannons. Racing through the water at top speed, the *Vicksburg* quickly closed the gap with the schooner and signaled her to "heave to." The *Agassiz* ignored the order and continued on course. A loud explosion sounded as the American gunboat sent a four-inch warning shot over the raider's bow that produced a geyser in the sea beyond. The *Agassiz* throttled back until it was dead in the water.

A launch was dispatched from the *Vicksburg* with a boarding party of rifle-bearing bluejackets. Motoring toward the *Agassiz*, they saw the Germans hard at work ripping up documents and tossing them overboard. By the time that the bluejackets reached the dormant schooner, the most incriminating papers were already beneath the waves, but enough evidence was seized to reveal the full extent of the plot. The American seamen discovered that the Germans had also made an attempt to destroy the boat's engines, ruining the magnetos in the process. The *Alexander Agassiz* was taken in tow by the *Vicksburg* as a prize of war. Its passengers were transferred to the gunboat, where the Germans were put in irons before being transported to California for trial. The American owner of the schooner, Maude Lochrane, was released after the authorities came to the conclusion that she was not involved in the scheme, but rather "a victim of Bauman's suave machinations."

The German plans for a reign of terror on the Pacific came to grief as the result of a casual conversation in a small Mexican restaurant in San Diego. Among the operatives of the San Diego APL Division was a handicapped newsboy. He had lost his legs in the army when, while changing from one train to another on his way to a new posting, he had slid beneath the moving wheels. To earn a living he became a "newsie," propelling himself along city sidewalks on a roller board while hawking newspapers. He came to the attention of a local APL officer because of his keen skills as an observer and his unusual intelligence—the newsboy spoke six languages. While eating at a Mexican restaurant one night, he had overheard a conversation in Spanish between a nearby party of Mexicans that revealed a wealth of information about German activities in Mazatlan. The newsboy sent a full report on the conversation to his APL lieutenant, which was forwarded to the San Diego APL headquarters and eventually to the Navy Department. It was this information that led to the wireless message to the *Vicksburg* and the undoing of the raider *Agassiz* off Mazatlan.

The handicapped newsboy that patrolled the streets of San Diego was typical of the operatives selected by the APL to monitor and investigate activities within a geographical territory. In the top-down personnel selection process of the League, "walk-in" members were virtually unheard of. Each city region was divided into divisions, and each division into districts. Every district had an APL captain in command who recruited as many working squads of operatives (assigned to lieutenants) as the size and character of his district demanded. One of the main responsibilities of a captain and his lieutenants was the selection of operatives that would be capable of the work at hand.

There were six qualities that the League sought in a prospective member, including loyalty, industriousness, an eagerness to contribute a large amount of their time to League duties, a willingness and ability to pay all personal expenses while on an assignment, and a readiness to contribute financially to support of the organization. These qualities were all prerequisites, but they would be nullified if the candidate lacked the most important quality that the League demanded: judgment. After meeting the basic qualifications, additional unique characteristics that would be of value to the League were taken into account—a skill or talent that would enhance their ability to collect information, such as foreign language ability, a special occupation, familiarity with a city area or neighborhood, or ownership of a motor car or boat. The wealth or social position of a candidate had no impact on the selection process; likewise, politics, religion, lodge affiliations, and similar criteria were not a factor in determining whether a prospective operative would be admitted to the League. As a result, the composition of a district's membership was typically highly diverse. Company presidents and office clerks, judges and mechanics, salesmen and janitors—all levels of social strata joined together in a common bond of patriotic service. All enlisted voluntarily with the knowledge that they would receive no pay and recover no expenses for the hours that they devoted each week to the work of the American Protective League.

Being asked to volunteer did not necessarily mean that a prospective candidate would pass the APL selection process. Only one in five candidates reviewed would eventually become a member. The remainder were rejected for a variety of reasons, such as being overly driven by the desire to carry a credential card or badge, being unable to devote enough time to League affairs, or showing a lack of discretion. As a final step before admission, the candidate's background would be investigated by a League operative.

Bernard Lichtenstadt, the man whose papers and League credentials were discovered in the Knoxville attic, provides a good example of the characteristics that the APL sought in an operative. Bernard L. Lichtenstadt was born on September 24, 1889, and grew up in an upper middle class German-American Jewish family in North Chicago. Bernard's father, Charles Lichtenstadt, moved to Chicago from New York in the late nineteenth century drawn by the opportunities to be found in the growing Midwestern metropolis. Charles found employment as a textile claim adjuster and eventually represented a number of eastern US textile mills. He also invented a textile waterproofing process and formed his own company to produce it. Both Charles and his wife, Arabella, were the children of German-Austrian immigrant parents, and it's likely that Bernard spoke the German language as well. The Lichtenstadt family lived on the edge of the Ravenswood section of North Chicago, which saw a tremendous influx of German immigrants during the turn of the twentieth century. Along the North Oakley Street neighborhood where Bernard was raised, over half of the residents had been born in either Germany or Austria. Following high school, Bernard Lichtenstadt attended law school, and, after earning a degree, opened a law office in the Shoaff Building in nearby Fort Wayne, Indiana. It was there that he met, courted, and married his first wife, Lillian Friedman, who was employed in Fort Wayne as a clerk at the well-known Wolf & Dessauer department store. A year later Lillian gave birth to a daughter who they named Rose Marie. Likely due to the need for a more certain and stable income stream to support his young family than could be obtained at his fledgling law practice, Lichtenstadt took a position as a traveling salesman with Pomeroy Brothers, a manufacturer of men's clothing, motoring to work in Chicago each day from his home in Fort Wayne.

Then the country went to war. On June 5, 1917, Bernard Lichtenstadt appeared at the Fort Wayne city hall to register for the draft. The twenty-seven-year-old claimed, and received, a draft exemption based on being the sole provider for a dependent wife and child. Lichtenstadt was typical of the men who would eventually join the American Protective League: young men of draft age like himself who were held at home due to family obligations, or men who were past service age who would otherwise have enlisted and were now searching for an alternative means to serve the war effort.

In August 1918, Bernard Lichtenstadt was approached by an APL member and volunteered to join the League, becoming Operative Number 7292 in the Chicago West Division, District 15, commanded by Captain C. R. Taylor. With the mission of the League being to report on disloyal or enemy activities and violations of the country's war codes, as well as to investigate all similar matters referred to it by the Department of Justice, Lichtenstadt's history and personal attributes made him an ideal candidate for becoming an APL Operative. He had grown up in a German-American household, was familiar with the language, and as a long-time local resident could circulate throughout the

German neighborhoods of Chicago with ease. He was a trained lawyer and understood the rules of evidence. As a traveling salesman with a motor car, he also had great mobility and could justify his presence in any area of the city while conducting an investigation.

On August 21, 1918, Lichtenstadt visited the nondescript brick office building at 130 North Wells Street that housed the satellite headquarters of Chicago's West Side District 15 to formally join the organization. Entering Room 1103, he met his Lieutenant as well as Captain Taylor and Lewis Bulkeley, the assistant inspector of the West Division who during the day worked as a broker for a dried fruits company. With a handful of other recent volunteers, Lichtenstadt took the oath of membership that was required to be taken by every individual that joined the American Protective League:

> I, Bernard Lee Lichtenstadt, a member of the American Protective League, organized with the approval and operating under the direction of the United States Department of Justice, Bureau of Investigation, do hereby voluntarily swear:
>
> That I am a citizen of the United States of America; and that I will uphold and defend the Constitution and Laws of the United States against all enemies, foreign and domestic, and will bear true faith and allegiance to the same at all times as a true and loyal citizen thereof.
>
> That I will give due time and diligent attention to such service as I shall undertake to render; and that I will execute promptly and to the best of my ability the commands of my superiors in connection therewith.
>
> That I will in all respects observe the rules and regulations, present and future, of this organization; and that I will promptly report to my superiors any and all violations thereof, and all information of every kind and character and from whatever source derived, tending to prove hostile or disloyal acts or intentions on the part of any person whatsoever and all other information of any kind of interest or value to the Government.

That I will not, except in the necessary performance of my duty, exhibit my credentials or disclose my membership in this organization; and that I will not disclose to any person other than a duly authorized Government official or officer of this organization, facts and information coming to my knowledge in connection with its work.

That the statement on the opposite side of the membership oath form, by me subscribed, is true and correct.

That I take this obligation freely, without any mental reservation or purpose of evasion; and that I will well and faithfully discharge my duties, as a volunteer for the defense and preservation of the United States of America, so help me God.

After taking the oath of membership, Lichtenstadt paid the $1 initiation fee required of every Chicago APL member that was collected to offset the fixed expenses of the division. He was then instructed to visit the APL Bureau of Membership in Suite 1135 of the Peoples Gas Building, where he was issued APL commission card number 7292 stating that he was an operative of the American Protective League, "organized with the approval and operating under the direction of the United States Department of Justice, Bureau of Investigation." Lichtenstadt also received a compact black leather credential card case manufactured by the George Seeley & Sons Company of Milwaukee, and a copy of the Chicago Division Operative's Handbook with his card number written on the cover. The handbook was a small pamphlet that fit behind his commission card in a pocket of the leather card case, and provided guidelines on APL operating procedures, rules of conduct, and included a concise summary of the federal laws that APL operatives were to enforce.

Shortly after the League was formed in 1917, nickel-plated badges were offered to members at a price of 50¢ each, imprinted with their rank and the legend, "American Protective League: Secret Service." At that time, the expression "secret service agent" was popularly used to describe any government agent, whether with the Department of Justice, US Secret Service, Immigration

Bureau, or the US Post Office Department. However, the "secret service" legend on these badges became such a cause of contention between the Treasury Department, under which the US Secret Service was organized, and the Justice Department, under which the American Protective League operated as an auxiliary, that by the fall of 1917, "Secret Service" labeled badges were no longer issued to League members. In late 1918, a new gold-plated brass badge was offered to APL members at a price of $3 each, imprinted with their individual rank and the legend, "American Protective League: Auxiliary to the US Dept. of Justice." When it was necessary for a League member to identify himself while entering an establishment on official business, contacting police, or placing a request to examine records, members were instructed to show their commission card instead of a badge. If a badge was to be displayed, it could be exhibited in a leather case provided by the League to permit a more professional presentation.

To manage and communicate with the legions of operatives, on one night each week every squad was required by APL regulations to meet with their lieutenant at a time and place arranged by the lieutenant. The first order of business at these meetings was a roll call of the operatives present, followed by an inspection of badges, commission cards, and operative's handbooks. This was followed by the reading of new APL bulletins and a discussion of cases. A written report that listed all members present and the fact that each was in possession of their handbook, badge, and card, would then be hand-delivered to the district captain by the squad's lieutenant.

Shortly after becoming a Chicago Division operative, Lichtenstadt received rudimentary training in detective work and the art of intelligence gathering. Most APL members had no previous law enforcement experience, but as a collective they were imaginative, intelligent men of good standing, and highly dedicated (which was why they had been chosen to join the League by their bosses, colleagues, or acquaintances), and they could learn by doing. Some members enjoyed a level of wealth or position that enabled them to devote all of their time to urgent cases. Instead of waiting for official approval to requisition an automobile, they had a car of their own to use. Without having to think about seeking expense approval, they would simply spend their own money to get the information that they needed. At a moment's notice, these businessmen could draw on a wide circle of friends and business associates for inside facts that would have taken a professional detective many days to secure.

At the district's school of instruction for new operatives, Lichtenstadt learned about the League's organizational structure as well as the elements of espionage laws and other war measures. He was instructed in the fundamentals of shadowing a suspect, the details of selective service regulations, the principles of law and evidence, and various other subjects required to carry out assignments as an operative. Most APL divisions did not have a formal training school for operatives. To make up for the lack of a structured training program, "the cleverest government operatives available and experienced city and private detectives talked to groups of captains and lieutenants, and these passed along the information to their men. A. Bruce Bielaski, Chief of the Bureau of Investigation, Department of Justice, was quick to recognize the possibilities of the League. Everywhere his organization gave invaluable aid and cooperation in training League members."

Officers and operatives were told to always remain aware of the fact that they were acting in the interests of the Department of Justice of the United States and to conduct themselves with dignity, tact, and discretion. They were to refrain from using words or engage in conduct that would in any way bring the government or the organization into disrespect. Voluntary submission to authority was a basic principle of the League. "The orders of the Chief must be obeyed, and any member failing or refusing to execute such orders or to conform to the practice and policy of the local branch will be subject to dismissal."

As New York APL Operative Brett Page observed, "No man who could not or would not live up to the spirit as well as to the letter of his oath was permitted to carry his credentials. 'Get good or get out' was the way one Inspector put it. And every man who couldn't 'get good' surrendered his card and badge."

Operatives were instructed to protect the identity of an informant if they happened to know it. It was unfair to an informant, they were told, to disclose his identity without permission and would prevent the League from receiving additional information from that informant in the future. They were taught that it was difficult to match wits with a suspect in order to trick him into disclosing his attitude toward the United States. They were told to secure that information from other sources. If the services of an operative who could speak a foreign language were needed, they should contact their lieutenant or phone the district office. Their captain could then assign an operative who spoke the required language to assist them. Most importantly, they were not to be afraid to ask for advice and assistance from their lieutenant or fellow operatives. The Division Inspectors frequently pointed out, "co-operation brings results."

There were many sources of information available to help APL operatives in conducting an investigation. To start with, they could use the regular city channels of information. If the operative obtained a name without an address, he was told to go to the nearest telephone directory or city directory. Sometimes a telephone number was known and the name of the party unknown; reference to the numerical telephone directory could locate this. Sometimes the business of a subject might be known and his address unknown, in which case it might be found by referring to the classified business telephone directory or the city directory. A subject might conduct business in the city but live in the suburbs; therefore, numerous suburban telephone directories were kept in the central office for reference. Chicago Division operatives were also instructed to use the "Book of Chicagoans," a directory that contained the personal history of many persons prominent in the city. In this book they could find the name, address, age, nativity, parents' names, education, business, and clubs of those individuals listed.

Additional, more specialized information was available at the district level. Each captain maintained a scrap book that contained the bulletins and orders that he had written and copies of bulletins issued by headquarters. Operatives were required to be aware of everything in the bulletin book. Each captain also maintained a news scrapbook containing clippings from local newspapers on people and matters of interest to the League. Operatives were instructed to familiarize themselves with this book as well, since often information that matched up with cases being investigated appeared in newspapers and was sometimes overlooked. If it was necessary to find out who owned a certain piece of property and that information could not be readily found through ordinary channels, operatives were to see their lieutenant, who could obtain information on the ownership of any piece of property through League sources. The League arranged for credit reports on individuals and firms to be made available to operatives for free. Operatives were also told who to contact to obtain information on parolees. For information on Chicago parolees, Lichtenstadt was instructed to contact Mr. Reed, parole agent at the Central Howard Association, 440 South Dearborn Street, Telephone, Harrison 511, who kept records on Chicagoans that had been released from jail on parole.

Although a small number of female investigators existed in the League and many women worked as office support staff, the enrollment of female members was officially frowned upon. Conforming to a popular belief that would keep women out of the workplace for decades, the national directors advised division chiefs that "the enrollment of women in the American Protective League is contrary to the national policy of the organization. While we are readily able to see the real service that might be performed by certain carefully selected women, we are forced to adopt the above attitude toward their enrollment in order to prevent disorganization among the male members." A particular concern was that if one man's wife was admitted to the League but another man's wife was rejected, it would lead to conflict between members.

In June 1918, the American Protective League began publication of an official newsletter called *The Spy Glass*. Copies were shipped in bulk to APL chiefs every other Thursday for distribution to their men at a price of 5¢ per copy or $1.30 for a one-year subscription. *The Spy Glass* contained articles explaining the latest war code regulations, administrative methods, "how to" investigative tactics, and general news articles from League divisions around the country. Oftentimes, issues included "wanted poster" information about fugitives or other individuals of interest to the government.

When making inquiries, operatives were taught that discretion was essential, as noted in *The Spy Glass*:

> In making an investigation it is important not to rush in precipitately and disclose the purpose of your inquiry. In questioning janitors, real estate people, etc., who may know about a man's residence, circumstances, etc., it is well to be reasonably sure such people are not pro-Germans. Sometimes you run across one who is, and it is better not to question him too closely for fear he will 'tip off' your subject and thus make your inquiry much more difficult—or even make it impossible to get any tangible results. Be sure you're safe, then go ahead.
>
> In investigating a man's business connections it is well to ascertain who his associates are and whether they are likely to be people you can talk to. If he is connected with a bank or business industry, call up the central [League] office and find out who is the captain of the squad of that industry, and go to him for assistance. The same practice is sound in getting information from hotels.
>
> In approaching a subject or source of information under cover, you may represent yourself as:
>
> - An automobile salesman.
> - A representative of a credit bureau.
> - A representative of an insurance company.
> - A representative of a food conservation committee.

- A representative of a charitable organization.
- Salesman for Liberty Bonds.
- Salesman for Thrift or War Savings Stamps.
- Reporter obtaining writeups.

Any one of these camouflages must be used with care, however, and on your own responsibility.

The operatives had access to the most advanced surveillance equipment of the day, including a box-like, takedown electronic camera for use in surreptitiously photographing a suspect's documents, and the dictagraph, a primitive recording device that could be placed in a suspect's room to secretly record conversations. Operatives were cautioned, however, that no dictagraph should be installed, telephone wires tapped, or similar methods employed without special authority. The necessity for obtaining this information first had to be reported to their chief, so that arrangements could be made through proper authorities to secure legitimate information. Chief Bielaski maintained a confidential arrangement with the telephone companies under which the Bureau of Investigation was supplied with information on all matters that passed over their lines related to the war. APL Chiefs were advised by Bielaski to make a similar arrangement with local telephone companies so that "information on matters of real importance" could be obtained, with the understanding that it would be kept entirely confidential. Information that had been telegraphed by suspects was more difficult to obtain, since the telegraph companies were loath to provide *anyone* with telegram copies. Once again, the bureau had a special arrangement with the telegraph companies under which special agents would be provided with telegram copies upon special request for the duration of the war. League officers in need of information that had been telegraphed were advised to make their request to the telegraph company through a BOI special agent. For obtaining postal information, the Justice Department also had an agreement with the US Post Office whereby the return and forwarding addresses of a suspect's incoming mail could be similarly obtained by special agents. Local postmasters were advised that this information was also to be provided to APL members. Apart from information legitimately obtained from telephone companies, telegraph companies, and the Postal Office, the warrantless break-in and search of a suspect's vacant room to obtain information was a common practice of APL operatives.

The lessons that Lichtenstadt learned at the district training school were reinforced by the guidelines contained in his operative's handbook. The APL Operative's Handbook had been created by the National Headquarters staff in 1917 to assist League members in handling their assigned cases. First distributed by Charles Daniel Frey to the Chicago Division, the operative's handbook provided basic information on the rules of evidence, an overview of the various war laws and regulations, and approved procedures to follow when conducting an investigation. The handbook ensured a measure of operational standardization within each division and across the organization as a whole. The following excerpts detail the course of action that a League investigator was expected to follow when carrying out an assignment.

OUR PURPOSE

The primary purpose of this organization is that of investigation. It is of the utmost importance that investigations be conducted in a thorough and business-like manner, so that the evidence so obtained can be made use of in the best possible way. Very often cases which on the surface appear to be more or less unimportant, on investigation lead to important conclusions. The facts should be obtained as fully as possible, and no avenue of investigation should be permitted to remain unexplored as long as the facts remain wholly or partially uncovered.

EVIDENCE

Evidence is all the means by which any accusation is established or disproved. The best evidence is proof which is so convincing in itself that it indicates that there are no more original sources of information. For example, the best evidence of the guilt of the subject accused of manufacturing bombs would be the testimony of witnesses who saw the subject actually doing the work. Further, the witness must testify from his own knowledge of the facts in dispute. For example, John tells Mary that Sam made a certain statement or violated a certain law. The testimony of John would be evidence; the testimony of Mary would be hearsay only and not evidence. Mary could not be a witness in a criminal prosecution; John would be a good witness. The purpose of the operative is to provide for the government good witnesses. Such evidence as you can obtain may be backed up by a preponderance of evidence of slight nature.

It is not always possible for the operative to obtain conclusive, indisputable proof, but it is essential that you obtain evidence from every available source.

You are to get evidence to prove the guilt or innocence of the subject or the truth or falsity of the charge. It is therefore to be constantly borne in mind (1) that a person is presumed to be innocent until he is proven guilty; (2) that action by the Government may depend on the evidence included in your report; and (3) that the evidence that you obtain should be sufficient to convince an unprejudiced mind

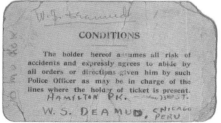

Among the items discovered in a Knoxville attic in 2008 (clockwise from lower left): a photograph of Operative B.L. Lichtenstadt taken in the 1940s, an APL operative's handbook, commission card and case, and Chicago Police Department Reporter's Pass issued to alias "William McCormick."

Advertising Executive Albert M. Briggs, the founder of the American Protective League. Photograph taken in 1918.

The National Directors of the American Protective League, April 1918 (left to right): Charles Daniel Frey, Albert M. Briggs, and Victor Elting.

FRANK L. GARBARINO
SPECIAL AGENT IN CHARGE

TELEPHONE WALNUT 4001
MAIL ADDRESS P. O. BOX 451

Department of Justice
Bureau of Investigation
ROOM 325 POST OFFICE BUILDING
PHILADELPHIA, PA.

July 27, 1917.

TO WHOM IT MAY CONCERN:

This is to certify that Mr. George W. Lukens of Philadelphia has been designated by the officers of the American Protective League to visit cities in the vicinity of Philadelphia, to organize local branches of the said League.

You will please co-operate with him and extend to him such assistance as he may require.

Very truly yours,

Frank L. Garbarino

TD/AG.

Agent in Charge.

The Justice Department in Washington directed Bureau of Investigation field offices around the country to render assistance to APL officials in organizing local divisions. This letter of introduction was written by the BOI Special Agent in Charge of the Philadelphia field office for use in organizing local branches of the League in the Philadelphia area.

Orchestrators of the German sabotage campaign in pre-war America (clock-wise from upper left): Ambassador Johann von Bernstorff, Captain Franz von Rintelen, steamship line detective Paul Koenig, and military attaché Franz von Papen.

The Ford Motor Company's Highland Park plant was the largest manufacturing complex in the world and a prime target for enemy sabotage.

Four hundred APL industrial division operatives were secretly located throughout Ford's Highland Park facilities to maintain vigil against sabotage. "There were tentacles of the APL organization reaching into every department . . . "

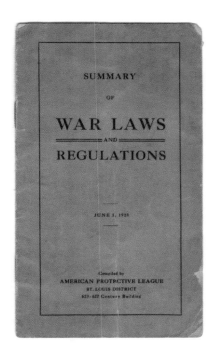

Registration Certificate (Draft Card) and Classification Card of Operative Lewis Clare Phillips. Draft registrants were grouped into classes from Class I to Class V based on their suitability for military service. Class I was composed of able-bodied single men; when this class was exhausted, local draft boards were to call up men from each successive class. Married with a dependent wife, Phillips was placed in Class IV. Among the many reasons that registrants were caught without their draft card was that it had been left at home for safekeeping or had disintegrated over time after being carried in an open pocket.

A War Regulations handbook published by the St. Louis Division of the American Protective League.

A handbill advising the public to be prepared for the national draft registration of September 1918.

The schooner *Alexander Agassiz*, clandestine raider. A German plot to use the *Agassiz* to terrorize Pacific shipping was averted through information obtained by an APL San Diego Division operative. Note the U.S. Navy officer on deck in the foreground and rifle-bearing seamen. *Inset:* The *Alexander Agassiz* was captured by the *USS Vicksburg*.

Four German deckhands captured on the *Alexander Agassiz* stand in irons aboard the *Vicksburg* before being transported to San Diego for trial.

Commission card of Operative Edward J. Baxter, 35-year-old Secretary-Treasurer of the John Anisfield Company, a large apparel maker in Cleveland, Ohio.

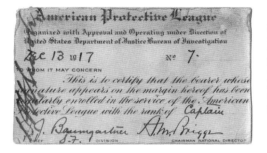

Commission card of Captain Dwight Milton Swobe, a 41-year-old Railway Manager with the McCloud River Railroad Company in San Francisco, California.

Commission card of Operative Lewis Clare Phillips, a 29-year-old Contracting Engineer with the Phillips Company in Chicago.

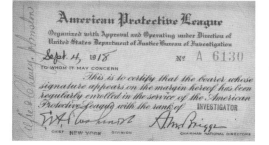

Commission card of APL Operative ("Investigator") Alfred Cheney Johnston, 33-year-old staff photographer for the Ziegfeld Follies.

In June 1918, the American Protective League began distribution of a bi-weekly newsletter *The Spy Glass*, which included suggested methods for conducting investigations and general news of interest to League members.

1917 Model APL badges and leather badge case. Lieutenant's badge shows 90+ years of tarnish.

APL New York City Division clerical staff transcribing operative's reports before distribution for review to APL headquarters personnel. Carbon copies were also forwarded to the Justice Department.

The records department of the APL New York City Division. APL investigative records were maintained at the division level as well as in a master file at the Department of Justice in Washington.

Smoke from the explosion still heavy in the air, Government agents and American Protective League members survey bomb damage outside the Federal Building in Chicago.

Gold-plated 1918 Model APL badges issued to the rank of (from left to right): Operative, Lieutenant, Captain, and Chief.

APL founder and National Director Albert M. Briggs sits at his desk in the League's Washington headquarters during the final days of the war.

"Certainly the most industrious person I have ever met..." National Director Charles Daniel Frey at work at his desk in Washington. He wears a black armband in memory of his late brother, Corporal Harry Frey, killed in France in August 1918.

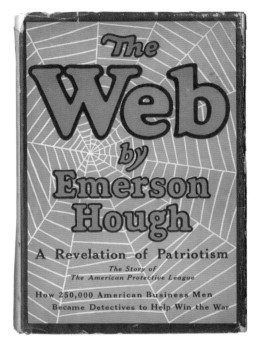

The cover of *The Web*. Published in 1919, the authorized history of the American Protective League was written by a best-selling author of western fiction.

The APL Chicago Division awarded honorable discharge certificates to its 12,000 members. Operative Bernard Lichtenstadt's honorable discharge certificate.

American Protective League

District No. 15, West Division

CHICAGO, ILL. January 31st, 1919

Opr. B. Lichtenstadt,
848 Montrose Blvd.,
    City.

Dear Sir : --
        This is the last day of life of the American
Protective League. The organization has indeed had a glor-
ious existence; it has played an important, even a noble part,
in the contribution of our country to the great war.

        The record of the League will ever fill a brilliant page
in American history. Its members have unselfishly performed
a fine patriotic duty, frequently at great sacrifice to
themselves and their families.

        The work of the League, as a whole, will no doubt be
recognized, but we, your former and present Captains, who
have been in constant personal contact with you during this
trying period, wish to take this opportunity of expressing
to you our deep appreciation of your efforts, your sacrifices,
and your achievements.

        You personally have contributed to the high standing and
character of District 15, a company which had no superior, if
it had an equal, in the entire League. Your record in the
district is one of which you may be justly proud.

        Let us hope that the friendships formed may be lasting,
and that the passing years will see us as closely bound
together as we are to-day.

        We could not fittingly close this letter without a word
of appreciation for the dear ones at home; the wives and
mothers, who perforce have been neglected during these months.
They too have made their sacrifices; they too have been soldiers;
and we salute them respectfully, reverently.

                    Sincerely yours,

Lewis E. Bulkeley   *C. Taylor*
Assistant Inspector.   Captain

Room 1103,
130 N.Wells St.,
Chicago,Ill.

            Mr. B. Lichtenstadt,

                848 Montrose Blvd.,

                        C ity.

It was a common practice for local division officers to send letters of appreciation to their men after the League's dissolution. This letter was sent to Bernard Lichtenstadt by Captain Taylor and Assistant Inspector Bulkeley to thank him for his service.

A somber group photograph of the National Directors and their support staff taken at the end of the war in front of the American Protective League National Headquarters in Washington. Within weeks the League would be disbanded.

beyond a reasonable doubt. Two witnesses are better than one.

A careful study of the law applicable to the case you are investigating will assist you to understand what evidence is required and what is evidence in the case you are working on. In this connection your attention is called to the Digest of Federal Statutes issued by this organization in July 1917, and also to "Laws and Proclamations" found in the Operative's Handbook. Each operative must understand these laws.

No investigation, other than that necessary to establish a clear complaint, should be undertaken until after a complaint has been turned in, checked, and assigned for active investigation.

HOW CASES ORIGINATE

Cases requiring investigation come to the organization in three ways:

1. Through complaints turned in by members.
2. Through complaints turned in by people not members of the organization.
3. Through complaints referred to the organization by the Department of Justice.

A diligent and constant watch on the part of operatives and officers for matters which should be reported for investigation is no less a duty than the active investigation of cases assigned to the operatives. Your company will be effective very largely in proportion to your careful watch of your district. Complaints from operatives should be transmitted in the regular course through lieutenant and captain, except in matters of extreme necessity.

THE HANDLING OF CASES

A case well thought out before being acted upon is half finished. Obviously no time limit can be set when report must be completed unless especially instructed by the lieutenant. The work of the organization contemplates that the operative start the investigation the day he receives the assignment.

Many times the Department is waiting for a report on the particular case you have, before taking action on some other cases on which your case has a bearing. Promptness therefore is vital.

If you are called out of town, notify your lieutenant who will advise you whether the case can stand the delay. A permanent record is kept of the date the case is given to the operative and the date returned. See that your interim is as short as the nature of the case will permit.

CASES FOR INVESTIGATION

It is difficult to give a definite set of directions for the handling of any particular kind of case. Operatives, when in doubt, must confer with their lieutenants who can at all times confer with the captain.

OPERATIVES AND METHODS

NEUTRALITY CASES*

What is wanted: In a neutrality case there is usually a charge made by some informant. That charge should be proved or disproved thru evidence and testimony. If, in the course of that investigation, the operative finds that the subject is loyal to the United States, he should investigate to find out in what respect the subject is disloyal.

METHODS IN NEUTRALITY CASES

1. Ascertain through list of voters in local office whether subject is a voter or not.
2. If the subject is not a voter ascertain whether he has registered as an alien. This can be obtained from the Alien Registry list in the central office.
3. If unable to find subject's name in either place notify your lieutenant who will find out for you whether subject has a voter's record or not. Do not delay in your investigation pending the report whether subject has voting record or not.
4. Secure what information regarding the subject you can from the neighbors of the subject.
5. Ascertain business and get what information is possible from business acquaintances.
6. Investigate the relatives and acquaintances of the subject.

---

*Investigation of Disloyalty—see Chapter 8 "Disloyalty is Now a Crime!"

7. Conduct the above investigation in such a manner that the subject will not know that he is being investigated.
8. Note that if a neutrality case is assigned to you, the subject is in effect paroled to you for observation and you should make reports regularly (once a week is the rule) until the case is ordered closed. Keep the subject under observation.

CHARACTER AND LOYALTY CASES**

What is wanted: Information that will give subject's general reputation as bearing on his loyalty, integrity and character. Character and Loyalty investigations are most important. Very often important decisions depend upon the result of the investigation.

METHODS IN CHARACTER AND LOYALTY CASES

1. Ascertain whether subject is a voter thru voting list.
2. Ascertain if he is an alien thru Alien List in central office.
3. If not a voter or an alien, see your lieutenant who will be able to ascertain for you whether he has a voting record but do not delay the case while the voting record is being obtained.
4. Secure what information is possible from neighbors of subject.
5. Find out business of subject and secure what information is possible from business acquaintances.
6. Investigate the relatives and acquaintances of subject.

** Background checks—see Chapter 7 "In Government Service"

7. Under no circumstances must the subject know he is being investigated without permission from the captain.

FALSE EXEMPTION CLAIMS

What is wanted: Evidence to prove the truth or falsity of the claims of the subject (draft registrant) for deferred classification.

METHODS IN FALSE EXEMPTION CASES

1. Information will be supplied to you as to classification by the Exemption Board and status of the subject by central office.
2. Find out from neighbors and acquaintances of subject the truth of the exemption claim.
3. If claim for deferred classification is on account of physical disability see subject's doctor. Also find out from subject's neighbors whether physical ailments are known.
4. If subject has life insurance policy, see his application for it.
5. If claim is on account of dependents, find out members of immediate family, their occupations, earning power, and whether or not any of them have a bank account or investments or independent income. If subject claims he is supporting a brother below 16 years or a sister below 18 years of age, get proof of their ages. Find out if dependents live with subject or not.

RED CROSS CASES

<u>What is wanted:</u> Most Red Cross cases are stories detrimental to the Red Cross. Stories such as this are particularly malicious, and the story should be investigated very thoroughly so that it can be proven or disproven. Also find out the origin of the story and the character and loyalty of those concerned in spreading it.

The APL Operative's Handbook provided step-by-step instruction for a novice investigator to follow. In an account written shortly after the war, New York operative Brett Page describes the trepidation that he felt as he embarked on his first assignment, and the guidance obtained from his Operative's Handbook:

This particular case seemed strangely different from any of those that I, in the company with other new members, had read about and had been carefully lectured to on 'the proper ways to proceed upon.' This case was 'my' case. It seemed very different from a mere hypothetical case. My faith in the lecturers was gone. My confidence in myself was shaken. And then—I remembered the little book of instruction that nestled just back of my member's card in the credential wallet. With trembling fingers I extracted that tiny pamphlet. Hiding it in a morning paper, I stood on the corner with the elevated roaring overhead, and read it from cover to cover . . . Instantly I was transformed, from a despairing patriot without an idea in the world (to one assuming the pretense of) the suave representative of a benevolent corporation insistently pursuing a lady to whom we panted to present four dollars and nine cents overcharged at some dim and distant date . . . The course of reasoning was so clear, so straightforward, and so perfectly plausible, that I smiled with confidence as I restored my precious pamphlet to its resting place. Then I took a deep breath, boldly marched down the street, mounted the steps and rang the doorbell.

After completing an assignment, operatives were instructed to make a full and exhaustive written report on the assigned case, to sign their name and badge number to the report, and to deliver it in person to their lieutenant - never to send it by mail. They were told to bear in mind that the person reading the report at headquarters would typically not be familiar with the case and therefore they were to be precise and accurate regarding all details. "Leave nothing to be assumed. Give the names and addresses of the persons from whom you obtain information so that they can be located. Leave out personal opinions in your reports. The evidence that you have obtained thru your investigations should be sufficient to enable the authorities to judge the case." The forms that were used in making official reports conformed to the record system used by the Department of Justice, and carbon copies of all APL reports and records were forwarded to the Bureau of Investigation. Eventually a complete record of every case investigated by the American Protective League was maintained in the Justice Department master file in Washington.

The following is an actual report prepared by APL Operative No. 229 of the Minneapolis Division describing his actions to locate and apprehend a British army deserter. It provides a good example of the detail expected of League operatives when preparing a written report of their assigned cases.

Report Made By:	Place Where Made:	Date When Made:
No. 229 APL	Minneapolis	7-16-1918

RE: SERGEANT FRED GREENE, Deserter from the British Army

On the afternoon of July 7th at about 3:30 Headquarters gave me the following information: "Sergeant Fred Greene of the

British Army is a deserter, and an officer has been sent from the British Headquarters in Chicago to effect the delivery of him to that office, and he (the officer from Chicago) has requested this office to endeavor to effect the arrest of Sergeant Greene. He lives at 629 Grand Avenue and the house was searched this morning. He was not there and the wife would give no information. She was very indignant. Will you endeavor to bring him in?"

Immediately I got into communication with several operatives, Nos. 154, 244, 328, 209, and 284.

No. 154 and I were on watch at a little after four o'clock, staying a little ways, a block or so, from the house. We realized that the husband was not in the house and that we must locate him through the wife. At about 4:45 Mrs. Fred Greene came into the front yard with a bright red coat on. She evidently suspected officers being on watch, and immediately returned to the house, either changed her clothes or simply removed the coat, but she came out in a dark dress and walked up and down the street for quite a while. Not observing anyone, she left the house, going down towards 22nd Street.

By this time No. 328 had arrived and I asked him to follow her. She went into a nearby grocery store, did not telephone anyone from there, simply purchased a few groceries and returned to the house. While she was away No. 224 arrived, and I asked him to endeavor to enter the house just across the street from the Greene house, which he did. In a little while Mrs. Greene returned and I told No. 224 to remain there until she left the house. I then left to get a bite to eat, expecting to return at 7 o'clock, but did not get there until 7:05. At 7:00 again Mrs. Greene left the house. No. 224 immediately asked No. 209, who had just arrived, to follow her, which he did very successfully. She took the streetcar at 22nd Street and Lyndale and left it at Hennepin, about 5th Street, very hurriedly purchased a suit case, and again took the street car towards the Great Northern Station; entered the station and was in the ladies' waiting room only about ten minutes. During that time she was in the telephone booth a very few minutes. From the waiting room she went to the checking room and checked the suit case. A porter, at the request of No. 209, secured the number of the check.

In the meantime, No. 209 had sent for me, and as we hurried to the station he described the boarder at the Greene house. Just after we arrived she left the station and boarded a Monroe and Bryant car. We followed the car. She left it at Franklin Avenue. I followed her for two blocks and saw her enter a drug store on the corner of 18th and Lyndale, and in about five minutes entered the store. She was standing there with another man, whom I recognized as the boarder who had been described to me. I then asked No. 209 to watch them closely while I communicated with the Chicago officer. I told him it was my opinion that they expected to meet Fred Greene and that on account of their suspicious actions we could probably force some desirable information from them. Also, that if he would come, I would arrest them.

He was there in a short time and in the meantime I had placed them under arrest and started an examination. A package was in the possession of the young man, whose name I could not learn. It proved to be the military cap of Fred Greene. Mrs. Greene refused to deliver to us the check belonging to the suit case and flatly stated that she did not know where her husband was, but that she thought he expected to go to Chicago. The young man also denied having any knowledge of his whereabouts. We started the automobile for the station, but had only gone a little way when, under pressure, she finally said that she expected to meet her husband there about 8:30, and the young man finally owed up to it too, so we immediately returned to the drug store.

I then instructed No. 209 to proceed to the station with the Chicago officer and Mrs. Green to get the suit case, which we later found contained Fred Greene's uniform, and which had been worn by Mrs. Greene under her clothes while on the way to the station, and removed them into the grip while she was in the telephone booth. The grip was checked, evidently that Mr. Greene might get the clothes later.

I, with the young man known as "the boarder," remained at the drug store. I placed him on the outside, directly in front of the store window, with instructions to notify me at once should Fred Greene appear, which he promised me to do. I remained out of sight. About 9:45 a party, whom I recognized as Fred Greene, appeared. The man did not give me any information. I happened about that time to be quite close to him, and asked him if [it were] Fred Greene and he practically made no answer, but I took charge of him and soon found that it was Fred Greene. We held him until No. 209 had returned from the station with the suit case and the other people, and then took Mrs. Greene to her home. She had threatened to kill herself and said that she had a gun to do it. She rushed into the house ahead of No. 209, into the bed room, closed the door and said the first man that came into the room she would shoot, but No. 209 told her to open the door immediately. She did, and he removed the bullets from the gun which she had in her hand, and on request left it with the young man boarder. We then delivered Fred Greene to the County Jail with instructions to deliver him to Sergeant Morton, the officer from Chicago, the following morning. At Sergeant Morton's request, No. 209 assisted him the following evening to deliver Mr. Greene at the station.

After being assigned to his squad and completing the required training, Bernard Lichtenstadt, Operative Number 7292 of Chicago West Division, District 15, would have begun to receive his first case assignments. Since no Chicago Division members are still alive and no firsthand written accounts remain in existence (all records of the APL's Chicago Division were burned in 1919), it's impossible to discover today what duties Lichtenstadt carried out during his APL service. However, since the League's primary rule in assigning cases was to choose the operative whose personal characteristics, social, professional, or business connections would ensure success with the least effort and in the shortest space of time, it's possible to deduce the type of cases that Lichtenstadt would have been assigned. As a second generation German-American from Chicago's Ravenswood area, Lichtenstadt was a prime candidate for cases requiring investigation of hostile or "disloyal" acts by German-Americans or Alien Enemies. He would also likely have been tagged for assignments that required locating draft delinquents, deserters, or unregistered alien enemies within the German community. A telling clue to Lichtenstadt's duties during the fall of 1918 is the reporter's pass that was found among his League effects. Dated September 1918 and issued to Lichtenstadt under the alias "William McCormick of the Evening American" by the Chicago Police Department, the pass enabled Lichtenstadt to pass through Chicago police lines wherever formed and to present himself as a reporter. This would have been extremely useful if, for example, he were assigned to monitor the radical gatherings still being held throughout Chicago at the time, such as the enormous meeting of 12,000 radicals and socialists that took place at the Coliseum on November 17, 1918. Since no Chicago Division records remain, no one will ever know.

Although the majority of League investigations consisted of hours spent examining records, observing suspects, and questioning neighbors and acquaintances, the potential for danger could be real. One afternoon in November 1917, APL Operative C. H. Keelor, Operative Logan, and a Mr. Sprague of the Justice Department were in one of the roughest parts of Philadelphia attempting to locate four men alleged to have been involved in a series of robberies of black army soldiers and other servicemen. They obtained information that one of the men they were looking for was Charles Seamore, who used the aliases "John E. Manuel" and "Puerto Rico." Working the neighborhood, Keelor and Sprague had just entered a saloon when a burly black man walked in and was hailed by the owner with the greeting, "How're you doin' today, Puerto Rico?" Keelor walked over to the man, tapped him on the shoulder, and asked to see his draft registration card. Immediately Seamore sprang into action like a wildcat, kicking Keelor in the leg and punching Sprague in the face, knocking him to the ground. Then, leaping away from the fallen pair, Seamore reached inside his coat and pulled out a .38 revolver, which he used to cover his exit from the saloon.

Once outside, Seamore raced northeast on Lombard Street. APL Operative Logan, who was positioned across the street, gave chase while being fired upon, apparently by a confederate of Seamore. Keelor and Sprague, by this time having recovered from the initial confrontation, ran out of the saloon and also lit out after Seamore. During the course of the pursuit, Seamore turned and aimed his revolver at Sprague who was armed with a heavy holster gun. Sprague was able to get off a shot first, killing Seamore with a bullet through the heart. When the trio searched the fallen bandit they discovered that in addition to his revolver, Seamore was carrying a sharp razor knife, a quantity of .38 ammunition, and a draft registration card showing that he had registered using an alias. A later investigation of the incident would justify Sprague's action as self-defense.

The operatives of the American Protective League were capable, well-organized, and dedicated in their desire to support Uncle Sam's war effort. In addition to their primary responsibility of carrying out assignments for the Department of Justice, they would soon be relied upon to assist a host of other US government agencies and departments in enforcing the war codes.

CHAPTER 7

IN GOVERNMENT SERVICE

It had been a busy afternoon at the Federal Building in Chicago, with a steady stream of visitors passing through its arched entranceway. The six-story gray stone building was a commanding structure in downtown Chicago, the seat of federal government power in the city. It occupied an entire city block and was topped by a golden dome with the American flag proudly flying overhead. Outside, where a few days before a large crowd had gathered to witness 95 IWW members taken to prison after sentencing, the sidewalks now teamed with pedestrians on their way to visit the many office buildings located in the area. Across the street, a war bond committee sold war savings stamps to a group of women and children standing beneath colorful canvas war banners.

The Chicago Post Office was located on the ground floor of the Federal Building. It was the busiest time of the day at the post office and hundreds of customers were lined at the stamp windows, or stood at the writing desks or letter registry. In the midst of the bustling activity, no one noticed the man as he walked into the post office. He was probably dressed like any other businessman of the day, a dark gray cloth suit, white shirt with starched collar, vest with a gold watch chain protruding from the pocket, and a black bowler hat atop his head. His left hand gripped a simple cheap suitcase of the type that every business traveler carried. He smiled casually as he walked through the busy post office, his face registering not the slightest trace of concern. It was a tremendous act of self-control since he knew that contained within the suitcase he was carrying were three wire-wrapped steel cylinders filled with nitroglycerine that would explode in less than an hour. Based on a later analysis of the bomb fragments, the cylinders were eighteen inches long by six inches wide, plugged at either end, with detonators wired to a central battery and a mechanical time clock. When a wire attached to the minute hand closed a circuit at exactly 3:10 p.m., the bomb would detonate. With a relaxed stride, the man that no one noticed walked to one of the writing desks, leaned over, and slid the suitcase behind an open radiator. Then he calmly exited the post office and disappeared into the passing throng of pedestrians . . .

As the bell in the dome of the Federal Building sounded at 3:10 p.m., the bomb exploded with a deafening blast. The radiator was torn from its fastenings and hurled twenty feet into the street where it killed a passing horse. A young woman named Helen Michike who happened to be walking with her sister past the entranceway was killed instantly. Another woman who was passing the British recruiting mission opposite the Federal Building was blown through a plate glass window by the blast. Great slabs of marble were torn from the sides of the building and flying fragments of stone, glass, and wood injured people in every direction. The patriotic banners of the War Bond committee across the street were torn to shreds by shrapnel. The windows of the neighboring Edison and Marquette buildings were blown out. The force of the explosion knocked hundreds of people from their feet. Injured and uninjured alike fled the building in a panic, some screaming in terror.

The epicenter of the explosion, the Chicago Post Office, was heavily damaged and littered with wreckage and debris. Clerk

Edward Kolkow was killed when the wall between a corridor and the general delivery room collapsed on top of him. Letter carrier William Wheeler was fatally injured. The remaining postal employees miraculously survived, including sixteen-year-old substitute letter carrier and future cartoonist Walt Disney, who had just finished his day's work and narrowly avoided being killed. All told, five people died in the blast and seventy-five were injured.

The tremendous roar of the explosion was heard all around the Chicago Loop. Among the first to arrive at the building and render assistance were hundreds of American Protective League members, their badges pinned to the outside of their coats. A newspaper account describing the scene marveled at how quickly the APL men had arrived, "as if summoned by telepathy," the reporter being unaware that the Chicago headquarters of the secret organization was in a building located less than a block away. Within half an hour of the bomb exploding, the APL's Chicago Division had mobilized over 1,500 men for duty. Large numbers of reserve police also arrived, and police lines were soon established half a block from the building on all sides. No one was allowed to enter or leave the building.

Responsibility for the explosion was immediately directed at the Industrial Workers of the World. "This outrage, in my opinion, was inevitable as an act of reprisal on the part of the I.W.W. following the sentencing of nearly a hundred of their members," declared Phillip J. Barry, the acting chief of the Bureau of Investigation's Chicago field office. "We are certain that the I.W.W. committed this deed." The courtroom of Judge Kenesaw Mountain Landis, in which the 95 IWW leaders were convicted and sentenced, was on the sixth floor of the Federal Building. William "Big Bill" Haywood, the organization's general secretary-treasurer and one of those recently sentenced to twenty years in prison, was actually on the eighth floor of the building with his lawyer filing court papers at the time that the explosion occurred.

On rush orders, the Chicago headquarters of the IWW on West Madison and Thorp Streets were raided by federal agents and American Protective League operatives. Nine Wobblies were arrested including Pete Dailey, a former member alleged to have made threats against the government following the trial; James Connelly, said to have connections with the IWW who was found on an upper floor of the building after the blast; and a man named Wilson, a secretary of the IWW reported to have been seen in the Federal Building foyer a few minutes before the explosion. A number of other suspects were apprehended by Bureau of Investigation agents and APL operatives who raced in automobiles from one location to another in the hours following the bombing. When questioned about the government's plans for bringing the culprits to justice, Acting Chief Barry commented, "In all, there are about 1,500 operatives working on the case. Many of these will be from the American Protective League. All persons known to be radical will be brought in and questioned. Visits will also be made to the haunts of people who are known to have sentiments against the war. Several arrests have been made and we are questioning the prisoners as fast as we can." Throughout the night, an army of Chicago Division operatives scoured the city, raiding the locations of any organization known to be hostile to the government. "Bring them all in, men and women alike," were the orders of those leading the investigation. But despite an extensive investigation that resulted in a handful of arrests, no one was ever tried for the bombing of the Chicago Federal Building on September 4, 1918, and the crime remains unsolved to this day.

Following the explosion at the Federal Building, officials of the United States War Exposition contacted the APL to request assistance in preventing a similar tragedy. The US War Exposition was a huge fair organized to build wartime morale among the populace. Held in Grant Park, the scene of the anti-war riot the previous year, the fair took place between September 2 and 15, 1918, and proved to be a popular attraction, with over two million attendees paying the twenty-five cent admission fee. The exposition featured a "no man's land" of trenches and barbed wire replicating a battlefield in France; mock battles were staged twice a day for the spectators. There were simulated infantry charges against enemy positions with soldiers going "over the top" firing blanks from rifles and machine guns, while tanks clanked across the landscape and military biplanes roared overhead. The exposition also included exhibitions of the latest Allied military hardware and captured German armaments. Following the bombing of the Federal Building, the fair was seen as a prime target for attack by antiwar radicals, and the organizing officials sought help from the Chicago APL Division to avert a similar tragedy. Over a period of eight days following the Federal Building explosion, the League maintained a roving patrol of 250 operatives that moved through the crowds each morning and afternoon, on the watch for any sign of suspicious activity. There was none, and the war exposition concluded as a great success, clearing a $318,000 profit for the country's war effort in ticket and concession sales.

The US War Exposition in Chicago was not the only time during the war that League members performed police patrol duties. Early in the summer of 1918, a system of nightly American Protective League crime watch patrols was established in downtown Minneapolis. The original intent of the patrols was to acquaint Minneapolis operatives with all of the various conditions of work encountered by the League and to provide them with specialized on-the-job training. Each APL district in Minneapolis was given three nights of patrol duty each month. The captain of a district and his entire corps of operatives would be on duty from 7:30 to 11:30 every tenth night. District 1 operated on the first of the month, District 2 on the second, and so forth. The eleventh district worked every Saturday night when the street crowds were the largest. The operatives worked in squads of two and three men each, some squads concentrating on draft evaders, others on bootleggers unlawfully furnishing liquor to soldiers, along with other violations. As the summer progressed, the Minneapolis operatives gained experience in many phases of law enforcement. A night rarely passed without one or more important arrests being made, and the entire membership of the Minneapolis Division soon became well acquainted with the downtown business and social structure.

To manage the nightly patrol system, a special headquarters was established in a central downtown Minneapolis building where the captain in charge directed operations. From this vantage point he could keep railroad stations, hotels, cafes, saloons, and other public places under continuous surveillance, and also had members constantly on call to meet any emergencies that might arise during the night. Squads of operatives were frequently dispatched from this branch headquarters to various parts of the city to apprehend law breakers, and several well-known criminals were arrested. According to the Minneapolis Division's "Summary and Report of War Service":

> It is a notable tribute to their courage and efficiency that there was not a single case of extreme violence during the period of the League's activities. Men recognized by police officials everywhere as dangerous were apprehended with the same ease that persons that had offended unwittingly were taken. Of the latter class many were helped to clear their records and were reestablished as good citizens. In its work the League employed all of the scientific, as well as the ordinary devices utilized in the detection and conviction of violators and evaders of the law. Dictaphones and disguises were used, and miles were covered and hours were spent in skillful "shadowing" and similar work.

A considerable number of bootleggers were apprehended by the nightly patrol system. Operatives would walk the streets in the districts where this traffic in liquor was going on. Seeing soldiers and certain types of civilians in conversation in a dark doorway or an alley, in nearly every instance, was evidence of a transaction whereby the civilian was to get liquor for the uniformed man [a violation of federal law at the time]. Generally the soldier or sailor would first be seen to give money to the civilian. The usual course of the latter was to the nearest saloon, from which he would return with liquor, which he gave to the man in uniform. After the operatives had witnessed the passing of the liquor, they would take the soldier and civilian into custody, holding the soldier for the military police from his detachment, and placing the customary charge against the civilian. Most of the latter readily pleaded guilty.

Cleveland, Ohio, was another city in which the American Protective League patrolled the streets to maintain law and order. In December 1918, Cleveland was in the midst of a well-publicized crime wave that had shaken public confidence and the general sense of well-being. During the preceding three months an epidemic of crime had erupted in the city resulting in four murders and scores of holdups and robberies. In just a single week in December, "automobile bandits," stickup men, and burglars had netted over $5,000 from various heists and holdups, killed one saloon keeper, wounded another, robbed twenty-seven people at gunpoint, burglarized eleven homes, and shot two policemen, one fatally. To help fight the growing crime spree, the chief of the APL's Cleveland Division, Arch C. Klumph, a successful retail lumberman and founder of the Cleveland Rotary, offered the services of the American Protective League to the Cleveland police. Accepting the assistance of the League, Chief Smith issued an urgent appeal "to every reputable citizen to lend a hand in ridding the city of burglars and gunmen." Soon a fleet of automobiles manned by police and American Protective League operatives armed with rifles and shotguns were patrolling the streets of Cleveland each night in an effort to run down the bandits and robbers. These mobile APL/police units were stationed at every police precinct in the city and began their motorized tours shortly after sundown. The orders that they had been given were clear: "If necessary, shoot to kill . . ." Cleveland Division members continued to participate in these joint crime watch patrols until the end of January 1919.

In addition to its primary function as an auxiliary of the Department of Justice, the League supported many other federal agencies in enforcing a variety of new government war regulations. The APL had begun working with the Military Intelligence Division (MID) of the War Department shortly after the country entered the war. In addition to providing assistance in protecting war production, pursuing draft delinquents and draft evaders, and aiding draft registration drives, the League also investigated cases involving individuals impersonating army officers, military bribery, theft, embezzlement, and fraudulent requests for furloughs. APL operatives conducted over 30,000 "character and loyalty" investigations ("background checks") of applicants for officer commissions, as well as of individuals pursuing overseas service in the Red Cross, YMCA, Knights of Columbus, Jewish Welfare, and Salvation Army. Local APL divisions also provided the MID with reports on any rumors circulating in their communities that would be harmful to the prosecution of the war.

In March 1918, the War Department requested that the American Protective League obtain public donations of photographs, drawings, and pictures of bridges, buildings, towns, and localities occupied by German forces in France, Belgium, Luxemburg, and the area of Germany north and south of Hamburg for use by Army Intelligence. To ensure maximum results, the APL's National Headquarters immediately issued a directive mobilizing all local divisions for the collection effort:

> To All Chiefs of the American Protective League—You will proceed at once to solicit through your organization, and in such other ways that commend themselves to you, all of the above materials including picture postals, photographs, half-tone reproductions, and other illustrative materials. The following methods will be found effective: 1. Wide publicity through the local press to the fact that the War Department has requested the American Protective League to procure the material from citizens throughout the country. The newspapers may invite citizens to make diligent search for such material and deliver it in person or by mail to a designated individual or office in your community which may or may not be the local

headquarters of the League . . . 2. Your leading newspapers will have in their library files or "morgue" a considerable amount of the material above described. They will doubtless be willing to give you originals or copies of these as a patriotic contribution . . . 3. In order to avoid disclosure of the personnel of your organization, you may wish to organize a special committee of citizens for the purpose; and you may enlist Boy Scouts, Camp Fire girls, and other organizations . . . 4. The active assistance of residents of your community who have resided or traveled in the countries indicated may be enlisted . . . This is a service which the American Protective League is peculiarly qualified to render in view of its widespread organization, but the total of the service will depend upon the diligence with which each local branch does its part.

According to *The Spy Glass* newsletter, "This effort resulted in the collection and shipment overseas of approximately five hundred packages of illustrative material containing an average of one hundred pieces each." In June 1918, the League received praise from the MID in a communiqué that quoted Colonel Nolan, chief of the Military Intelligence Force Overseas, as saying that the information provided was highly valuable and that "the citizens of the United States who donated the articles and the League which collected them have done something which definitely helps toward the success of the operations of our army."

In addition to work undertaken for the Department of Justice and the Military Intelligence Division of the War Department, the League also carried out assignments for the Fuel and Food Administrations, the Alien Property Custodian, and a host of the country's other government agencies and departments.

The United States Fuel Administration was an agency headed by Dr. Harvey A. Garfield, the purpose of which was to control the country's use of fuel (coal, oil, gasoline) to ensure maximum availability for the war effort. As American participation in the war gained momentum, the demand for fuel by military equipment manufacturers, the armed forces, and commercial shipping increased dramatically. At the same time, the winter of 1917 and 1918 proved to be one of the coldest on record, further stressing the nation's fuel supply. The country's coal consumption amounted to 650 million net tons in 1917, but the coal requirements in 1918 were expected to reach 735 million net tons. The difference would have to be made up both by expanded fuel production and by significant public fuel conservation.

In January 1918, Dr. Garfield announced a program of nationwide fuel conservation measures. With few exceptions, on every Monday of the week, no factory, store, office building, amusement facility, or saloon in the United States would be allowed to use fuel, and each would have to remain unheated. On Thursday and Sunday nights it would be illegal for any business to use external building lighting for display or advertising purposes, including store window lighting, electric advertising signs, and movie house marquees. The use of passenger elevators was restricted to certain hours of the day. Dr. Garfield also requested that no automobiles be used for pleasure rides on Sundays to further conserve the nation's gas supply to meet war needs. Public adherence to the new Fuel Administration regulations was vigorously enforced by the American Protective League. On "fuelless" Mondays, local operatives visited hundreds of public and private facilities to ensure compliance, often taking temperature readings within the buildings in search of violators. They were also on the lookout for "coal hoarding" during these inspections. On "lightless" Thursday and Sunday nights, League members took to the city streets to investigate violations of the lighting rules. During "gasless" Sundays, Leaguers would monitor streets, roads, and highways for pleasure drivers as well.

The United States Food Administration, headed by Herbert Hoover, issued regulations that were aimed at conserving wheat and meat products in order to increase the supply available for the army and America's European allies. To conserve wheat, food producers were required to use a specified percentage of substitute grains and cereals in their products. No hotel, restaurant, or club was permitted to use more than six pounds of wheat flour per ninety meals served. Wheat products could not be served unless ordered; bread and rolls could not be placed on a customer's table until the meal had been served and then only in individual portions. No sugar bowls were allowed on tables. Sugar could only be served in individual portions of restricted size. It was illegal for a retail outlet such as a grocer to sell more than two pounds of sugar to any one individual at any one time. To increase the available supply of meat, restaurants and hotels had to observe a specific number of meatless days per week during which they could not supply meat products to their customers. Similar to its monitoring of public compliance with the fuel regulations, the American Protective League also policed compliance with the government food regulations. At times, the entire membership of a League division would be called upon to check and report violations at bakeries, restaurants, and hotels.

The Alien Property Custodian, A. Mitchell Palmer, headed an agency whose purpose was to gain custody and control of enemy property within the United States. Palmer's position was created under the "Trading with the Enemy Act" that prohibited commercial activity of any kind with enemy companies or enemy agents during the war, whether in the United States or overseas. Before America entered the conflict, German-owned businesses such as the Hamburg-American Steamship Line had been virtual outposts of the German empire and were used to support espionage and sabotage activities within the United States. The US government recognized that during the war German and Austro-Hungarian firms could be used to wage economic warfare, working commercially against Allied war objectives. The Alien Property Custodian was empowered to prevent this by taking title to enemy-owned businesses. Palmer's organization seized a variety of German companies: the Bosch Magneto Company; the wharves and piers of the Hamburg-American line at Hoboken, New Jersey; the Foreign Transport and Mercantile Corporation; and assorted textile mills, breweries, mines, and a host of other concerns. German and Austrian business owners in turn adopted a variety of ploys to conceal their ownership in American firms. To avoid detection and loss of their holdings to the Alien Property Custodian, a common subterfuge was to "sell" interest in a company to an American caretaker, transferring stock in return for a promise of payment six months after the end of the war. (The stock would be returned to the original owner after the war and the transaction cancelled without transfer of funds.) Identifying concealed enemy ownership of American businesses would require significant detective work and the skills of a knowledgeable business analyst spending many hours poring through financial, legal, and business records—an ideal assignment for the businessman operatives of the American Protective League.

In August 1918, Palmer contacted the APL National Headquarters in Washington and requested that the League "aid him in the discovery, particularly in the smaller communities, of such enemy-owned concerns as were not yet in his hands." APL members were tasked with discovering the true ownership of suspected enemy-owned businesses, identifying any individuals acting as custodians of enemy-owned companies, and obtaining a complete description of the suspect properties for the Alien Property Custodian. By the end of the war, Palmer's organization would take custody to over $700 million worth of alien enemy business property. Some of these holdings were sold or operated by government appointees during the war, the proceeds being invested in Liberty Bonds. The remaining business and investment properties were retained by the Alien Property Custodian until the end of the war.

The American Protective League was a valued resource for an array of federal departments and agencies during the war years. As Attorney General Gregory noted at the war's conclusion, "upwards of *3 million* investigations have been conducted (by the American Protective League) for the Department of Justice, Military Intelligence, The Provost Marshal General's office, the State, Navy and Treasury Departments, the Food and Fuel Administrations, the Alien Property Custodian, and other Government bodies." This resulted in cases being assigned to the

League relating to a broad range of unlawful activities including espionage, sabotage, draft evasion, and illegal trade.

One sweltering August afternoon in 1917, an operative named Hastings was preparing to leave the N.Y. Division headquarters at 35 Nassau Street for the day when he was called over by the desk officer. A telegram had just been received from an agency in Washington requesting a "character and loyalty" investigation (background check) on an individual who had volunteered for private war work in France. Since the volunteer's references lived near Hastings's town, could he follow up on the request and interview them? Hastings readily agreed, and left in the company of another League operative named Lindley whom he'd previously consented to drop at home along the way. Traveling in Hastings's roadster, the trip was uneventful and the pair soon arrived at the hamlet where the references lived, a beautiful village with a number of large country estates. Hastings swung his auto off the main road and pulled into a railroad station to ask for directions to the two street addresses that he'd been given.

Lindley remained in the car while Hastings entered the station. The waiting room was empty except for an elderly man writing out a telegram at the ticket office window. Hastings walked across the room to where the man was standing and peered into the ticket office, but it was vacant, the stationmaster busy in the adjoining room checking in a trunk. Resigning himself to a longer than expected delay, Hastings turned and looked out at his car. As he did, the old man shifted his position to block Hastings's view of the message that he was composing.

The subtle gesture immediately drew Hastings's attention.

Waiting for the stationmaster to appear, Hastings discreetly examined the man in detail and noted that he had dirty hands and wore the rough work clothes of a manual laborer. Casually turning to take another quick look at his car, Hastings was able to catch a glimpse of the telegraph blank. The man's handwriting exhibited the sweeping curves of an educated writer, not the forced scrawl of a workman. Was it his imagination, or did it resemble the flowing characters of Germanic script?

The stationmaster soon came into view at the ticket window. Before Hastings had the chance to ask for directions, the laborer brusquely shouldered in front of him.

"Could you send this telegram please? I have the money all set—seventy-five cents."

He pushed a handful of change at the stationmaster, received a receipt, then turned on his heel and headed out the door. Hastings walked to the open doorway, gave a nod to Lindley, and signaled for him to follow the man who was now advancing down the road at a rapid clip.

The operative returned to the ticket window where the stationmaster was busily counting the words of the old man's telegram. *If only I could see what it says,* thought Hastings. It would be easy enough to contact a BOI special agent and obtain the text under an official request—but that would take time. He decided on a quicker route.

"Hello. I need to find a half-dozen connections. Would it be any trouble if I just step around and take a look at your Bullinger's Guide?" Hastings asked the stationmaster.

"Sure, come on in," the railroad man replied, still engaged with the telegram. "Make yourself at home."

Hastings entered the little ticket office and pulled the chained Bullinger's railroad connection guide onto the counter top. While pretending to study the guide, he was able to look over the stationmaster's shoulder and read the message.

The telegram was addressed to a woman in the Midwest and read simply:

"I am much better now. I should be able to get rid of the cane tomorrow."

The operative flipped through the connection guide a few minutes longer and returned it to the shelf. Then he asked the stationmaster for directions to the streets where the references for the overseas volunteer lived. After thanking the man heartily for his assistance, Hastings moved outside. He eagerly scanned every avenue of approach, but Lindley and the old man had long disappeared.

Walking to his car, Hastings wondered why the old man had bothered to conceal such a trivial message. The man obviously had no need for a cane—was it some sort of code?

Confident that Lindley would tail the mystery man to his destination and eventually turn up to report, Hastings drove off in his roadster to complete the assigned "Loyalty and Character" investigation. Then he returned home and waited.

It was eleven o'clock at night before Lindley rang his doorbell, weary and covered with dust.

"Why the devil did you have me shadow that old codger?" he demanded.

Hastings quickly related what he'd seen at the station.

"For the love of Mike, he's just a gardener!" Lindley responded. "Works at an estate ten miles from here."

"A gardener? Ten miles away—you mean you *walked* it?"

"More like marched it," Lindley replied. "We probably ended up hiking half-a-dozen miles more. He's in better shape than you'd think. Led me a merry chase all night—and then to find out he's just a blamed groundskeeper."

"There must be more to this," said Hastings. "Why didn't he send the telegram at a telegraph office near his place? Why did he walk ten miles to send a message like that?"

They pondered the situation for a few seconds in silence.

"You know, there's a great view of the ocean from the old man's greenhouse," reflected Lindley. "You can easily see every ship putting out from New York harbor . . ."

The pair agreed to continue the investigation the following day, a Sunday, by splitting up and canvassing the area where the man worked.

Hastings set off in his roadster shortly after daybreak. Driving straight to the gardener's estate, he parked his car beneath a willow grove less than a block away. Lindley had been right about the view from the greenhouse, it was a spy's dream come true. Every ship that moved in or out of New York harbor could be plainly seen with the unaided eye—freighters, ocean liners, barges, and in the coming months, troopships bound for England. As the morning wore on, under a variety of pretexts, Hastings questioned individuals throughout the neighborhood and learned that the gardener didn't have any friends. No one had even talked to him except one woman who thought him "a bit odd" and a native of Switzerland.

That afternoon Hastings met up with Lindley to compare notes. Lindley had hit pay dirt. He'd visited every telegraph office within ten miles of the residence where the groundskeeper worked. Two of the telegraph operators recognized the description Lindley had given them and volunteered that the man had come into their offices to send telegrams at different intervals, sometimes days, other times many weeks apart, to a man named James Hunt at a hotel on the New York waterfront. Neither operator remembered ever receiving a message for the old man in return.

With a solid lead to pursue, the pair cranked their cars and drove out to the waterfront hotel. They located the day clerk who advised them that there was no James Hunt registered. Assuming the pretense of a good friend trying to locate his old pal "Jimmy," Hastings questioned the night clerk and soon learned that Hunt was the wireless operator of an American coastal vessel. He also learned the name of the ship.

The two operatives suddenly realized that they'd come to the stage—or were perhaps already beyond the stage—at which regulations demanded that they report what they had discovered as a "new case" to division headquarters. They promptly reported their findings, and luck was with them. In those early days of the League, they were the APL members who lived closest to the suspect and were therefore assigned the investigation.

When Hunt's ship steamed through the narrows and docked at a side pier in New York harbor, Lindley was standing on the dock waiting to board the vessel. He immediately sought out Hunt and, displaying his APL commission card, advised the wireless operator that there was a small matter that needed clearing up at headquarters. Hunt readily agreed to accompany Lindley in a taxicab to the League office on Nassau Street. At the same time, Hastings paid a similar visit to the gardener and made the same request. The old man seemed very nervous at first, but agreed after some persuasion.

At division headquarters the two suspects were questioned in separate rooms, neither aware that the other was in the building. The interrogators began by confronting them with the entire series of telegram messages that the gardener had sent to Hunt, which the Bureau of Investigation had obtained for the League from the telegraph company. Each telegram contained a simple query regarding their health. No two were alike and the nature of the physical complaints varied widely. Both men claimed that the messages were related to a venture that they were partners in—the development of tin mines in South America. Their interrogators pointed out that communication about a routine commercial matter would hardly require such involved coded messages—if their story was true. Although both Hunt and the gardener continued to stick to their stories, the men running the interrogation were certain that something was being concealed.

Leaving the suspects alone for awhile, the examiners talked the situation over in the hallway. They decided to switch the men that they were interrogating. Each walked into the interview room where the other man waited, and with triumph written on their faces happily announced, "It's all over, the other man has confessed." At this, the gardener fell into deep despair and grew silent. But the wireless operator cracked at once.

"They're hidden in the hollow beam on the port side of my cabin—fourth from the first beam forward," Hunt exclaimed. "Please, if you get me off I promise, I'll never, *ever* smuggle another diamond again!"

Not an espionage matter at all, it turned out to be a case for the collector of customs. The message to the woman in the Midwest that had started the investigation was explained following an investigation conducted by the APL division in that state. The gardener had left his family to travel to New York, perhaps with the money used to finance the diamond purchases that Hunt smuggled in and sold at great profit due to the wartime economy. He had fabricated the story to his wife about being lame as an alibi for not forwarding household expenses.

Both the men, their confessions, and the evidence were turned over to the authorities before their trial on the charge of diamond smuggling . . .

Another case that began as an espionage investigation, before taking an unexpected turn, started in Cincinnati. On August 5, 1918, an emergency telephone call was received at the Cincinnati Division headquarters from an executive of one of the largest trust companies in the city, requesting that an operative be sent to the bank as quickly as possible. When the operative arrived and assessed the situation, it appeared that the bankers had indeed uncovered the trail of a German spy or saboteur. That afternoon a telegram had been received by the bank from the Empire Trust Company of New York City, authorizing $25,000 to be placed to the credit of one Frank Krueger. When Krueger arrived to withdraw the funds shortly thereafter, he immediately aroused the suspicion of the bank officials who were well-versed in the regulations of the Trading with the Enemy Act. Krueger was about fifty-five years of age and looked "typically German." The man was extremely nervous, which, when combined with an overanxiousness to display his naturalization papers proving American citizenship, led the bank officers to put off his request for the funds until after they had the chance to contact the League.

"I'm sorry, but we do not have $25,000 in available cash for you to withdraw this afternoon," Krueger was advised by a bank officer. "You'll have to return tomorrow. Where can we reach you when the money arrives?"

"I am staying at the Gibson Hotel," Krueger had replied.

The Cincinnati Division sent a message to the New York Division to investigate at their end, and then dispatched a team of operatives to the Gibson Hotel. Learning that Krueger was out, they searched his room from top to bottom and left undetected. Nothing in the warrantless search of Krueger's room threw any light on what the man planned to do with the currency or the purpose of his visit to Cincinnati. The operatives maintained surveillance at the hotel throughout the night, but nothing unusual transpired. It would just be a matter of time before Krueger called on the bank again to withdraw the funds.

The following morning the League acted. Krueger was taken to the Cincinnati field office of the Bureau of Investigation where he was questioned at length by the special agent in charge. Uncooperative at first, after two hours of interrogation Krueger finally revealed the story behind his urgent need for $25,000 in cash.

He had been born near Hanover, Germany, in 1863. His family emigrated to the United States when he was sixteen years old and settled in New York. Six years later he became a naturalized US citizen. Krueger eventually married and fathered three children. He made a living as a stone mason for ten years and then worked as a contractor for the next eighteen years. He was able to put away enough money to open a saloon and roadhouse in East Orange, New Jersey, which he operated for a time before moving to West Hoboken, where he retired. Krueger's retirement had been pleasant enough, until he was struck by a severe case of rheumatism. His physician recommended convalescence at a health resort in Mount Clemens, Michigan, where Krueger became a resident during the spring of 1918.

At the health resort Krueger made the acquaintance of two jovial and highly sociable gentlemen, Frederick B. Grant and Jack Connel. It was obvious to Krueger that both men were extremely wealthy, and after considerable arm-twisting he was able to draw out where their money had come from. Grant, who was the spokesman of the two, revealed that he was a successful coal operator in West Virginia, but most of his riches were the result of a system that he'd originated that made betting on horse races "a sure thing." Grant took Krueger aside, swore him to secrecy, and in hushed tones explained how the system worked.

A few days later, Krueger, Grant, and Connel left the health resort and traveled to the Vendome Hotel in Newport, Kentucky. The wealthy mining men took the retiree to a local pool room that fronted for a bookmaker, and sure enough, by employing "the system," Krueger won $25,000 in less than a week. When he attempted to collect his winnings, however, Krueger learned from the proprietor that, under the laws of the State of Kentucky, he could not withdraw the money unless he had an equal amount of money on deposit in the state. Krueger contacted his daughter in Hoboken and advised her that he needed $25,000 immediately to complete a business deal. He was able to raise some of the money himself, and his daughter secured the remaining amount through a loan from the Empire Trust Company.

Krueger concluded his story with an appeal to the Justice Department agents to allow him to be on his way so that he could withdraw the $25,000 and obtain his winnings.

The special agent in charge made a quick call to the state attorney general's office and the pool room was raided. The telephone and telegraph system that had greatly impressed Krueger when placing his bets was found not to be connected to any outside line. Huge stacks of currency that Krueger had glimpsed in the money room turned out to be paper from a New York telephone directory cut to the size of a dollar bill, stacked four to five inches thick with a genuine $100 bill placed on the top and bottom.

In spite of the evidence, Krueger's confidence in Grant and Connel was so great that it was only after hours of convincing by BOI agents and League officers that he accepted the fact that his "friends" had almost stolen his life's savings and agreed to provide testimony against them on the charge of fraud.

An unusual case in Minneapolis began during the second National Draft Registration Day on September 12, 1918. For this registration, the age range was expanded to include men from eighteen to forty-five years of age, and as a result over thirteen million men were registered for the draft that day. The entire membership of the American Protective League was mobilized to support the effort. Their orders were to assist the registration process, keep watch over the men waiting to register, and look for any individuals that had failed to register during previous registrations who were now subject to arrest for draft evasion.

In Minneapolis the largest crowds occurred in the early morning hours, before men went to work, when the columns of waiting registrants often extended for several blocks. At one of the busiest precincts in the city, the odd behavior of an individual standing near the front of the line soon caught the attention of two League operatives. The man's registration card stated his occupation as "iron molder," but to the operatives he looked more like an office worker than a foundry man. Instead of the tough-as-leather hands expected of a laborer who handled hot steel molds for a living, his hands were soft and unblemished. The operatives exchanged curious glances . . .

When the man departed the registration area, he was discreetly followed by one of the operatives. The remaining operative went to a pay telephone and called the manufacturing plant that the man had listed as his place of employment. He was informed that they had never heard of him. The deceptive registrant was eventually shadowed to a lodging house. After he entered the building, the operative who tailed him there phoned his captain and outlined their suspicions. Headquarters immediately sent additional operatives to the man's address. When they entered the lodging house they learned that the suspect had disappeared. Although at this point there was nothing concrete on which to base an investigation, the lodging house was placed under twenty-four-hour surveillance.

Five days passed and the man still had not returned, so the decision was made to search his flat. The team gained entry and explored his room, discovering a number of curious articles. There were blank checks that had been issued by banks in a handful of cities, several photographs of the suspect wearing a German army uniform, and letters and military pamphlets written in German. Raising the carpet in his room, they found an official United States Army discharge certificate blank. These discoveries stirred further concern among the League investigators. They carefully returned the items to the locations where they had been found and relocked the door to the room.

Surveillance was maintained for another seven days when, without warning, a man arrived at the lodging house and inquired about renting the room that had been occupied by the suspect. He was able to describe the room to the landlady in great detail. On instruction from the operatives, she agreed to let him rent the suspect's flat. The new boarder entered the room, where he was observed packing the effects of the suspect. Shortly thereafter, he left the boarding house carrying two suitcases containing the suspect's belongings.

Outside he was confronted by the team of League operatives. When they asked what he was doing, he stated that a man matching the suspect's description had given him $5 to go to the lodging house, rent the room, remove his belongings, and meet him at a certain spot the following morning where he would receive another $50 in cash.

The unwitting accomplice was held overnight and then released the next day to keep his appointment with the suspect. When the suspect arrived for the meeting, he was immediately taken into custody. The fraudulent registrant was unable to give any explanation for the photographs and documents that had been discovered in his room, and only after lengthy interrogation confessed to being a deserter from the United States Army. He also admitted to being an unregistered German alien and told League officials that he had deserted from the German army as well. The man could not account for his activities between the time of his desertion from the US Army and his capture in Minneapolis. He was carrying a significant amount of cash when arrested, but could not offer any proof of employment. The man was eventually turned over to the military authorities while the Department of Justice opened an investigation into whether he was still in the service of Germany.

Throughout the First World War, League members hunted for spies and saboteurs, searched for draft evaders and army deserters, performed background checks on officer candidates and civilian workers going overseas, and investigated the ownership of suspected enemy-owned businesses. The American Protective League would also be used to enforce the loyalty of US citizens . . .

CHAPTER 8

DISLOYALTY IS NOW A CRIME!

Tension was starting to build among the lawmen. This would be the most important arrest that any of them had ever made, and no one wanted anything to go wrong. They had been working the case for days, ever since the federal grand jury in Cleveland handed down the secret indictment. Now Eugene V. Debs, four times the Socialist Party's candidate for president of the United States (in 1912 he had captured over a million votes), an internationally renowned politician and labor leader, was going to be arrested under a federal warrant. The charges: ten specific counts of violating Section 3 of the Espionage Act, as amended by passage of the Sedition Act.

The team assembled by the Justice Department to apprehend Debs was sufficient for capturing an "armed and dangerous" fugitive: from the Bureau of Investigation, Special Agent in Charge of the Cleveland Field Office Bliss Morton and Special Agent John Sawken; from the Marshal Service, US Marshal Charles W. Lapp and Chief Deputy Marshal Charles Boehme. No photographs would be required to aid them in identification of Debs; like most Americans, they would instantly recognize the lanky, balding, and bespectacled Socialist leader from seeing his picture in newspapers and newsreels. The plan was to make the arrest in Cleveland on June 30, 1918, where Debs was scheduled to be the featured speaker at a huge gathering of Socialists at the Bohemian Gardens.

From the time that the indictment was returned, all trains into Cleveland were under the watch of federal agents. Despite the intense surveillance, Debs slipped into the city without interference, arriving on an early morning train from Indianapolis before disappearing into the crowded train station. The lawmen were not overly concerned about missing the chance to seize Debs on arrival since they knew where he'd be at 3:30 p.m. that afternoon—delivering his speech.

Shortly after 2 p.m., a reception committee of Socialists departed the Bohemian Gardens to pick up Debs, unaware that they were being tailed by a second car carrying Justice Department agents from a discreet distance. The Socialists drove to the Hotel Gillsy where Debs planned to stay during the Cleveland engagement. The agents watched Debs exit the hotel and get into the passenger seat. He was then taken on a brief tour of the West Side Boulevard. At precisely 3:20 p.m., the Socialist's car returned to the Bohemian Gardens where 3,000 enthusiastic supporters were waiting to hear Debs speak.

As the car drew to a stop, the agent's vehicle pulled in quickly behind it and a signal was given to the US Marshals waiting at the entrance to the Gardens. Special Agent John Sawken met Debs as he stepped out of the Socialist's car and introduced him to Marshal Lapp and Deputy Marshal Boehme.

"I'm glad to know you, Mr. Debs," said Boehme. "I have a warrant for your arrest."

Debs smiled at the agents and replied, "All right, I'll come along."

He was immediately escorted to the marshals' automobile and driven to the Federal Building. The arrest had been carried out so smoothly that few individuals among the throng waiting to greet Debs were aware of what had transpired until after Debs was gone. Later that afternoon, Debs was removed to the county jail to await arraignment. Justice Department officials were confident of the case that had been built against him, since extensive evidence of his guilt had been provided by their own auxiliary, the American Protective League. The charges were based on statements that Debs had made during a speech at the Socialist state convention in Canton, Ohio, on June 16 of that year.

The chief of the APL's 261-member Canton Division was Elton W. Partridge, an Ohio newspaper advertising executive. Anticipating that violations of federal law would occur at the Socialist convention, Partridge had ensured that thirty-four operatives from the Canton Division were in attendance. One of these, an expert stenographer, was actually on the speaker's platform near Debs and recorded every word that was spoken during his address. A complete transcript of the operative's report was forwarded to the US Attorney at Cleveland the same day, which later resulted in the secret grand jury indictment.

Following Debs' arrest, Edwin S. Wertz, US Attorney for the northern district of Ohio, announced, "No man is too big to be held responsible for his actions under the Espionage Act or any other law of the United States." Assistant US Attorney Joseph C. Breittenstein added, "Mr. Debs was indicted not as a Socialist but as a violator of the law of the United States because of the things that he said in his Canton speech."

What were the statements that Debs had made that led to his arrest? The heart of Debs' speech included the following:

> Comrades, friends and fellow-workers . . . I have just returned from a visit over yonder, where three of our most loyal comrades are paying the penalty for their devotion to the cause of the working class. They have come to realize, as many of us have, that it is extremely dangerous to exercise the constitutional right of free speech in a country fighting to make democracy safe in the world . . . If it had not been for the men and women who, in the past, have had the moral courage to go to jail, we would still be in the jungles.

When the Bolsheviki came into power [in Russia] and went through the archives they found and exposed the secret treaties—the treaties that were made between the Czar and the French government, the British government and the Italian government, proposing, after the victory was achieved, to dismember the German Empire and destroy the Central Powers . . . I have a copy of these treaties, showing that the purpose of the Allies is exactly the purpose of the Central Powers, and that is the conquest and spoilation of the weaker nations that has always been the purpose of war.

Wars throughout history have been waged for conquest and plunder . . . The master class has always declared the wars; the subject class has always fought the battles. The master class has had all to gain and nothing to lose, while the subject class has had nothing to gain and all to lose—especially their lives . . . They have always taught and trained you to believe it to be your patriotic duty to go to war and to have yourselves slaughtered at their command . . . Yours not to reason why; Yours but to do and die.

Rose Pastor Stokes!* . . . What did Rose Pastor Stokes say? Why, she said that a government could not at the same time serve both the profiteers and the victims of the profiteers. Is it not true? Certainly it is and no one can successfully dispute it . . . I want to admit—I want to admit without reservation that if Rose Pastor Stokes is guilty of crime, so am I.

They are continually talking about your patriotic duty. It is not their but your patriotic duty that they are concerned about. There is a decided difference. Their patriotic duty never takes them to the firing line or chucks them into the trenches . . . And now for all of us to do our duty! The clarion call is ringing in our ears and we cannot falter without being convicted of treason to ourselves and to our great cause . . . Do not worry over the charge of treason to your masters, but be concerned about

---

* Rose Pastor Stokes was a prominent Socialist orator convicted of violating the Espionage Act for writing a letter to the *Kansas City Star* that included the statement, "No Government which is for the profiteers can also be for the people, and I am for the people, while the Government is for the profiteers."

the treason that involves yourselves. Be true to yourself and you
cannot be a traitor to any good cause on earth.

For the crime of stating these words in public, Eugene Debs was
sentenced to ten years' imprisonment in a federal penitentiary.

America's entry into the conflict had triggered a national sense
of insecurity with regard to the country's ability to maintain a
popular consensus in support of the war. This was in part a reaction to the influx of European immigrants into the United States
at the turn of the twentieth century. The general belief was that
many of these immigrant groups, including German-Americans,
Austrian-Americans, and Irish-Americans, held a dual allegiance
both to their native land and their newly adopted homeland—
or remained fully dedicated to the land of their birth and would
present a security risk in time of war. The disparaging nickname
for such immigrants at the time was "hyphenated Americans."
As Teddy Roosevelt said, "There is no such thing as a hyphenated American who is a good American. The only man who
is a good American is the man who is an American and nothing else." By that Roosevelt meant that naturalized Americans
should be dedicated to the United States alone and not maintain
an allegiance to any other country.

Apart from their perceived menace as potential spies or
saboteurs, it was also believed that "hyphenated Americans"
presented a danger due to their propensity for "disloyal" talk.
This perception was reinforced by the political dialogue that had
taken place in immigrant communities across the country, before
America became involved in the war. When German or Austrian
forces won a victory or appeared to be gaining an advantage,
German and Austrian immigrants and their descendents were
quick to voice their opinions regarding the ultimate triumph of
the Central Powers. Following the United States' entry into the
war, these people became suspect.

During the prewar period, other groups spoke out against
America taking part in the European conflict—religious sects

like the Mennonites and Amish, whose creed espoused pacifism, or Socialists and radicals who viewed the war as detracting from the greater economic class struggle. With the American declaration of war, pacifist sentiments became "disloyal" and "pro-German." If someone did not want America in the war then they must want the Germans to be victorious. What had been "free speech" in peacetime became "dangerous seditious utterances" after the war began, aimed at inciting rebellion against the government and its war policies. This viewpoint was best expressed by Judge Kenesaw Landis in his summation before sentencing the IWW leadership in Chicago: "In times of peace, you have a legal right to oppose, by free speech, preparations for war. But when war has been declared, that right ceases forthwith."

It was strongly felt by a broad segment of the population that disloyal talk by "hyphenated Americans" and other "pro-German" sympathizers could significantly undermine the war effort. Seditious utterances could generate resistance to draft registration, encouraging young men of draft age not to register or appear for induction—to become "slackers." Disloyal talk could lower revenues from the sale of government securities—the Liberty Bonds and Savings Stamps needed to finance American participation in the war. It could increase the dissemination of false stories and rumors about the Red Cross, the living conditions of US troops in training camps and at the front, or the supremacy of enemy forces. Disloyal utterances by those of German ancestry or "traitorous" pro-German sympathizers could ruin the morale of soldiers and citizens alike and destroy America's ability to win the war (or so it was thought).

From its inception, one of the main functions of the American Protective League was to report all disloyal activities and infractions of the war codes. APL industrial operatives, the "eyes and ears" of the League, were ever vigilant listening for seditious or pro-German talk in offices, shops, and factories. After receiving Justice Department approval, APL investigative operatives were quick to follow up on complaints against German sympathizers, investigating all reported pro-German or otherwise "disloyal" statements. But until the spring of 1918 there were no federal laws that defined seditious or disloyal talk as a punishable crime. The original version of the Espionage Act passed in June 1917 was primarily aimed at spying activities. Its provisions relating to personal speech were restricted to individuals making false reports intended to interfere with the operation or success of US military forces, or for causing insubordination or disloyalty in the ranks—too narrow to punish most purveyors of disloyal comments. After passage of the Espionage Act, the Department .of Justice began to press for additional legislation to deal with the sedition and disloyal speechmaking believed to be running rampant throughout the country. The Sedition Act was soon introduced in Congress, but it languished in committee, stalled by advocates of free speech and a free press. Then an incident occurred that captured national attention and gave the legislation new momentum.

On April 4, 1918, a forty-five-year-old German immigrant named Robert Praeger made a speech to some miners in Maryville, Illinois, that was alleged to be socialistic and "disloyal." A mob quickly formed that attempted to seize Praeger, but he was able to escape in an automobile to nearby Collinsville. Several members of the mob followed him there and succeeded in raising another angry crowd in Collinsville that went to Praeger's home and dragged him outside. Praeger was forced to remove his shoes and socks, and then marched down the main street of Collinsville draped in an American flag while the mob sang the national anthem. Every few blocks the crowd stopped and forced Praeger to kiss the flag. Soon Collinsville policemen were able to intercept the crowd and rescue Praeger from the mob, which now exceeded 350 people and included many prominent citizens of Collinsville and the local area. Praeger was then placed in a cell in the City Hall jail. "While I was born in Germany I have been nationalized and I am for the good old U.S.A.," the alleged pro-German said to the policemen on duty. A few hours later the crowd, which had now swelled in size, gathered in front of City Hall and demanded that Praeger be surrendered to them. Collinsville Mayor Siegel appeared on the front steps of the building and pleaded with the crowd to "let the man have a fair trial." Inside, Praeger, who had been removed from his cell by the police and hidden in the basement, scribbled a note in German:

> Dear Parents and Carl Henry Praeger, Dresden Germany: I must on this the 4th day of April, 1918, die. Please pray for me, my dear parents. This is my last letter and testament. Your dear son and brother, Robert Paul Praeger.

Meanwhile outside, spotting an opening in the cordon of police, several men at the front of the mob made a rush toward the city hall doors, forcing the mayor and police officers aside. The crowd surged into the building and, calling out Praeger's name, began a search from top to bottom. They soon located the terrified immigrant hiding behind a pile of tiling. Praeger was dragged outside and, still barefoot, was led with a rope around his neck along the old national highway, past the outskirts of Collinsville to one of the largest trees in the countryside. Despite the huge mass of people, not a word was spoken by the crowd, and in silence the rope was thrown over a high branch. Praeger once again began to plead his innocence: "Please, I am loyal to this country!" The rope was pulled, and Praeger was lifted ten feet off the ground. A contingent of police from East St. Louis, racing across Illinois at high speed, arrived at the scene only to find Praeger dead, his lifeless body still hanging from the tree.

The next day Mayor Siegel and the Collinsville chief of police said that they were not inclined to take action on the matter since the killing had occurred two miles outside of the city limits. Mayor Siegel added that he "had found no evidence of disloyalty against Praeger." The mayor of Marysville where the disloyal comments that sparked the incident had allegedly occurred had no comment for reporters. But then, it was unlikely that he would, since the Marysville mayor had also been born in Germany and two months before Praeger's murder had himself been forced to kiss the American flag.

The lynching of Robert Praeger made newspaper headlines across the country and became a subject of discussion at President Wilson's cabinet meeting the next day. The shift from the more common "tar and feather parties" of alleged pro-Germans that had repeatedly occurred around the country to a hanging gave the government officials "grave concern as to what the future might bring forth if steps are not taken to prevent enraged Americans from taking the law into their their own hands." (A German named Frederick Wilhelm Gustave Ehlen was tar and feathered in Flint, Michigan, for making alleged pro-German comments on the same day that Praeger was killed.) Department of Justice officials made the remarkable argument that until the federal government was given the power to punish people for making disloyal utterances, it was feared that more lynchings would occur; only when Congress passed the still-pending Sedition Act, making it a federal crime to speak or write disloyal criticism of the United States during wartime, would the government be able to punish these disloyal acts and reduce the danger of mob violence.

This view was shared by the American Protective League. In a letter to the National Directors sent on April 3, Chief G. H. Walker wrote:

> The St. Louis District, American Protective League, wishes to give its hearty endorsement to the Bill reported by the Senate Judiciary Committee, supplementing certain provisions of the Espionage Act relating to disloyalty; and we beg to urge you out of our own experience, to emphasize the necessity for this additional legislation . . . Our files are full of cases of disloyal utterances of sufficient gravity to provoke breaches of the peace, wherein, by reason of the insufficiency of the laws to reach such conduct, no precautions have been possible, nor have the offenders been inconvenienced to the

slightest extent . . . There is no doubt in our mind that the inadequacy of the laws and regulations, coupled with the absence of vigorous enforcement, has contributed to a growing disrespect for authority on the part of a large body of persons . . . This has been strikingly emphasized (as you are no doubt informed from newspaper accounts) by the many incidents in which over-zealous citizens have taken the law into their own hands and sought to supply the deficiencies of the statutes.

A month after the Praeger hanging, on May 7, 1918, Congress passed the Sedition Act following a number of stormy sessions in which the legislation was denounced as tyrannical and threatening freedom of speech and a free press. Representative London had vainly sought to have the bill sent back to committee to restore an exemption from any penalty for individuals who "in criticism of the government speak the truth with good motives and for justifiable ends" and Representative Gordon complained that the Senate had placed language in the bill "which plainly is in violation of the Federal constitution guaranteeing free speech." Despite the rancor, the Sedition Act was passed by a vote of forty-eight in favor to twenty-six against along nonpartisan lines with many Republicans joining a majority of Democrats in supporting the legislation.

The Sedition Act became an amendment to Sections 3 and 4 of the Espionage Act and introduced the following new language:

Whoever, when the United States is at war, shall . . . say or do anything except by way of bona fide and not disloyal advice to an investor or investors, with intent to obstruct the sale by the United States of bonds or other securities of the United States or the making of loans by or to the United States, and whoever when the United States is at war . . . shall willfully utter, print, write or publish any disloyal, profane, scurrilous, or abusive language about the form of government of the United States or the Constitution of the United States, or the military or naval forces of the United States, or the flag of the United States, or the uniform of the Army or Navy of the United States, or any language intended to bring the form of government . . . or the Constitution . . . or the military or naval forces . . . or the flag . . . of the United States into contempt, scorn, contumely, or disrepute, or shall willfully utter, print, write, or publish any language intended to incite, provoke, or encourage resistance to the United States, or to promote the cause of its enemies, or shall willfully display the flag of any foreign enemy, or shall willfully by utterance, writing, printing, publication, or language spoken, urge, incite, or advocate any curtailment of production in this country of any thing or things, product or products, necessary or essential to the prosecution of the war in which the United States may be engaged, with intent by such curtailment to cripple or hinder the United States in the prosecution of war, and whoever shall willfully advocate, teach, defend, or suggest the doing of any of the acts or things in this section enumerated, and whoever shall by word or act support or favor the cause of any country with which the United States is at war or by word or act oppose the cause of the United States therein, shall be punished by a fine of not more than $10,000 or the imprisonment for not more than twenty years, or both;

When the United States is at war, the Postmaster General may, upon evidence satisfactory to him that any person or concern is using the mails in violation of any of the provisions of this Act, instruct the postmaster at any post office at which mail is received addressed to such person or concern to return to the postmaster at the office at which they were originally mailed all letters or other matter so addressed, with the words "Mail to this address undeliverable under Espionage Act" plainly written or stamped upon the outside thereof.

With the passage of the new legislation, American citizens and aliens alike lost the right to criticize the US government, the president, the draft system, or the armed forces for the duration of the war. To do so, whether intentionally or unintentionally, could result in prosecution for sedition in wartime. There were now two alternatives when talking about the war effort—voice support and approval or remain silent. Despite the loss of their constitutional right to free speech, both the Sedition Act and the home front war against the disloyal enjoyed a solid base of support among the general population. Public sentiment during this time of intense patriotism was against anyone who wasn't "100 percent American" and it was felt that loyal Americans had nothing to worry about from the new law. A typical expression of this attitude is described in the following newspaper editorial from the *Logansport* (Indiana) *Pharos-Reporter*:

> If you are loyal and your friends are loyal, what have you to fear from the espionage act? The espionage act has a penalty only for disloyal folks. Just be decent, loyal folks and you, as far as the operation of the penalty is concerned, will likely go through the entire war and not know what the provisions of the law are. An honest man might go through a whole life time and not know what the laws are regarding theft. Penitentiaries are made for criminals, and not one percent of Indiana folks even know what the institution at Michigan City looks like. Neither do they care anything about it. Laws against disloyalty have no terror for the loyal. So don't get scared or you will give the whole snap away.

Under the headline, "Disloyalty Is Now A Crime," the League's *The Spy Glass* news bulletin described the opportunities presented by the new measures:

> Signed by President Wilson on May 16, the amended espionage law opens a new chapter in the work of the American Protective League. For the first time we have an inclusive law under which to operate—a law broad enough in its scope and classifications to cover and define as serious crimes a multitude of offenses which were classed as minor by our peace-time code but actually offered serious hindrances to this country's

military operations and preparations. No distinction is made between the disloyal talk or act of a citizen and the hostile speech or deed of an alien, enemy or otherwise. The act or speech is the offense and whoever commits it must pay the penalty—though the law allows a good deal of latitude to the court in determining the latter. All this means a tremendous simplification of every member's labors.

League investigations of disloyalty originated in a variety of ways. APL Industrial Division operatives scattered across shops, offices, hotels, banks, and other enterprises around the country often overheard seditious utterances and filed a complaint. Reports on disloyal activity also came into League offices from the general public by way of a notification from the Department of Justice. For example, the Justice Department would send a request to the chief of a local division for information on "John Doe" from Mayfield, alleged to have made disloyal comments. Loyalty cases often originated from the public sending reports directly to the APL division office. Although the American Protective League was a secret organization from the standpoint of who was involved and where they were located, it often conducted extensive "public service advertising" to enlist the aid of the general populace in reporting disloyal activities. Local APL divisions posted advertisements in a variety of venues requesting that citizens report all cases of seditious and disloyal talk to the League. The Buffalo (New York) Division, for instance, issued disloyalty awareness posters in two sizes: a large 16" x 21" sign for use in street cars, store windows, and factory bulletin boards, and a smaller 6" x 8" version for use in elevators, public and club smoking rooms, bowling alleys, and "other places of general resort." In either version the tag line was the same: "Use your eyes and ears and report these people over your signature, to the American Protective League, P.O. Box 10, Buffalo, NY." League divisions also placed advertisements in local and regional newspapers to solicit tips from the public, such as the following ad that appeared on page four of the May 13, 1918, edition of the Greenville, Pennsylvania, *Evening Record*:

DON'T CRITICISE THE GOVERNMENT

FOR FAILING TO ROUND UP EVERY ONE OF THE TRAI-
TORS AND AGITATORS

YOU Are The Government

UNCLE SAM IS NO MIND- READER—HERE IS WHAT
YOU CAN DO

Show up the disloyal and pro-german propagandist. The man whose words the ntion show that he is trying to help Germany to win the war.

This is every American's business, and in this crisis every man, woman child stands FOR America or AGAINST her.

Do you part, and the work of those who are encaged in clubbing in the soldiers in the book will be minimized.

Write the facts in any case which has come to your attention give names of witnesses, SIGN YOUR NAME and mail to post office Box 152.

The names of persons giving information will not be disclosed if they so desire.

AMERICAN PROTECTIVE LEAGUE
(The Mennner County Civilian Braney, Bureau Of
Investigation, Department Of Justice)
Box 152, Greenville, Pa.

According to the League's authorized history, "much important information resulted from this practice." Another prime source of information was the US Post Office. Newspapers advised their readers that "the medium between the public and government secret agents for the transmission of information relative to seditious remarks and efforts to escape the draft is the city postmaster, who is receiving written messages daily from citizens furnishing clues."

Throughout 1918, complaints of disloyalty poured into the League from a range of sources—even religious clergy. In a letter sent to National Director Charles Daniel Frey on April

20, 1918, Bishop Theodore S. Henderson of the Methodist Episcopal Church in Detroit suggested that the League should investigate the alleged disloyalty of one of his ministers:

> I have been suspicious for a long time that one of our ministers, a member of the Rook River Conference, whose chief city is Chicago, Illinois ought to be looked up . . . This man has been holding a part-time professorship at Boston University in Boston, Mass., one of our Methodist institutions but has recently been engaged to become a professor in Union Theological Seminary, New York City. I refer to Professor Harry F. Ward, the author of certain books on the labor question, and whose writings and utterances in this time of crisis are, to my mind, decidedly dangerous. One of the bishops of our Church within forty-eight hours has told me that when the I.W.W. crowd were raided in Chicago, or indicted, he sent them a letter of sympathy and condolence. I do not know whether this is true but we ought to be able to find out. Will you take the matter up from the Washington end?

In investigations of disloyalty, as in all assignments that it carried out during the war, the American Protective League operated under the direction of the Department of Justice. An actual disloyalty case investigated in St. Louis, Missouri, shows how their relationship worked. One day a client visited the office of his lawyer, and after their business discussions had ended, remained to banter awhile during which he revealed that he had heard a German sympathizer say, "Every American child should have its neck wrung as soon as it is born. The German Army could rule the United States better than Wilson—and it will, too." During the course of their conversation, the lawyer was able to casually draw out the name and address of the offender, and the names of witnesses who had also heard the disloyal comments. After his client left, the attorney, who was a member of the League, prepared a full report of the incident on a blank form supplied by the Department of Justice and sent it to the captain of his unit, signing the report with his Operative Number. The lawyer was a member of an APL industrial unit, so his duty ended there, since industrial members were only allowed to gather information, not to investigate cases. The captain took the report to St. Louis Division headquarters, where it was reviewed by League officials who then forwarded it to the local office of the Department of Justice, Bureau of Investigation. There it was approved as a complaint worth investigating, whereupon the case was assigned by League headquarters to the operatives of an APL investigative unit. These operatives were tasked with obtaining affidavits to corroborate the hearsay information supplied by the lawyer. After several days of investigation, the evidence that they collected was dispatched to the Attorney General to determine whether to prosecute the lawyer's client for violating the sedition laws.

The amended Espionage Act not only made "disloyal talk" a federal offense, it also introduced harsh penalties for the expanded list of offenses. The Department of Justice and the American Protective League assiduously pursued complaints regarding sedition and disloyal activities, with the League conducting literally *millions* of investigations of alleged acts of disloyalty during the war. Whether a violator was arrested and tried in court for what they had said or written or just received "a good talking to" by a local APL officer (who would describe the penalties for disloyalty and advise the individual to remain quiet in the future) was dependent on the stance of the local APL division or the discretion of the investigating operative. The League's authorized history documents the wide range of punishments that could be imposed for "disloyal utterances." It also illustrates how far many League divisions strayed from BOI Chief Bielaski's 1917 directive that "great care must be taken that nothing is done to unnecessarily alarm aliens in this country or cause them any apprehension as to the fair manner in which they will be treated":

Oakland, California:	"Oakland Division dealt out its punishments to the enemy drastically.

Seventeen well-known local Germans, business and professional men, drank a toast to the Kaiser in the Faust Café, a German restaurant. The APL got the necessary evidence, and ten of these men were convicted of disloyalty. The court put the punishment at three months in the chain gang and a fine of $250 each."

Hickory,
North Carolina:

"We had no aliens—all native born American citizens . . . When we got to work, all the 'aginners' who were against the war got on the right side. Especially was this true after the amended espionage act went into effect. 'In my judgement,' said the Chief, 'the psychological effect of an organization that could be felt but not seen helped wonderfully in bringing to their right senses the small minority that were not right at the start.'"

Aberdeen,
South Dakota:

"Aberdeen, South Dakota must have been a good talking point for German propagandists, because it reports 122 cases of propaganda by word of mouth, and 128 cases of propaganda by printed matter . . . One (of the cases) . . . was president of the South Dakota German-American Alliance, and published a German language paper at Sioux Falls. He was charged with writing a letter which reads as follows: '*I have never given any declaration of loyalty and never will do it, nor subscribe to any Liberty Loan. The name is to me already an emetic because it is hypocritical and misleading. That a man buys perhaps* *bonds for business considerations, I can understand, but I myself couldn't do it without thinking that my $50 or $100 might perhaps buy the explosive which American accomplices of the allied plunderbund might throw on the house of my mother.'* He was sentenced to ten years in the Federal penitentiary."

Green County, Iowa:

"All quiet in this section. Very few Germans in our county. None showed disloyalty except one old German woman who wrote to her son, a missionary in China. Her family promised to keep her loyal."

Freeborn County, Minnesota:

"The loyal folks were so plentiful that if any pessimist happened to say the wrong thing about the Red Cross or Liberty Loans, he was promptly reported. A few fines of $500 each in the district court soon stopped all the disloyalty talk."

Cleveland, Ohio:

"A gentleman by the name of Joseph Freiheit—Freiheit means freedom in German—said that if sent to the army he would not shoot at the Germans. He advised his friends to do the same. He was brought to (APL) headquarters and reprimanded. The next day he committed suicide."

Sparta, Wisconsin:

"The cashier of a bank wrote a letter in which he stated his bank would not take any Government certificates. He gave as his reason that he was short of help, as one of his men was being held in the army against his will and 'against the wishes of the community.' He was spoken to."

White Sulphur Springs, Virginia:

"A baker of this town named Adolph held certain opinions which would not strictly classify as American. When asked to Purchase War Savings Stamps, he expressed himself as follows: 'To hell with your War Savings Stamps. If Uncle Sam didn't have money enough to finance the war, why did he go into it? When the American soldiers get to France, you'll find they won't do anything but run like hell.' In the US District Court at Charlestown, he confessed to a violation of the Espionage Act, was fined $100 and sentenced to two years in the penitentiary."

Bradford, Pennsylvania:

"Bradford operated under cover as much as possible. A good many townsfolk could not identify APL at all, although there were very few who did not know that there had been some sort of checking up of pretty much the entire population in matters of interest to the Government. This impression aided in suppressing a great deal of radical and seditious talk, and served as a warning to others not to begin that sort of thing."

An abundant supply of information on "disloyal utterances" was provided by the civilian committees selling government securities—Liberty Bonds and Service Stamps. Sometimes those being solicited supplemented their refusal to buy bonds with a remark such as, "I won't give money to help England suppress innocent Germany," or "America has no business in this war." Young men planning to enlist occasionally told draft authorities that someone had advised them not to enter the army or navy "because Germany was sure to win" or "American transports are certain to be sunk." Such offhand remarks would be reported to the APL and investigated by League operatives.

During the summer of 1918, reports arrived at APL headquarters from civilian Liberty Loan sellers and draft registration authorities in Ohio regarding alien activities at the Herrick mine of the Wheeling and Lake Erie Coal Company in Steubenville. The sixty mine workers at the Herrick mine were Austrian immigrants. During the Third Liberty Loan campaign, the Herrick miners had subscribed only $1,200, while other mines in the same vicinity, employing a like number of men, had subscribed as high as $18,000. According to the accounts provided, the Herrick miners reportedly spoke out against the Liberty Loan effort, urging other miners not to buy them and threatening those who did. The miners also defied the draft registration officials at Herrick, and when pressed by their foreman to register, several were alleged to have declared that they would *not* register, and further, would fight for no country other than Germany or Austria. Based on these allegations, the American Protective League surreptitiously infiltrated operatives into the Herrick mine workforce.

Several weeks passed, and on the afternoon of September 25, 1918, a convoy of automobiles from the Jefferson County War Board pulled to a stop at the Herrick mine entrance and a team of lawmen exited, including US Marshal Sam Loftus, US Commissioner N. D. Miller, Sheriff W. T. Baker, and Constable Edward Lucas. Also in the escort was a party of ten "Steubenville Minute Men" under the command of Colonel T. H. Loomis. The APL investigation into disloyal activity at the Herrick mine had been completed, and now every "pro-German" at the mine was a marked man. The Herrick miners were assembled by their company foremen, and Marshal

Loftus stood on one of the automobiles to address them. He announced that the men whose names he was about to call out would receive their pay first and were to step to one side. After the fifteen wanted men had been grouped together, they were surrounded by the "Minute Men."

"We are United States Marshals and you men can consider yourselves under arrest," Marshal Loftus declared.

According to newspaper reports, the remaining miners gathered around the officers appeared dumbfounded for a moment. Marshal Loftus addressed them next, praising them for their loyalty to the flag and stating that an example would be made of every "enemy sympathizer." The miners broke into a spontaneous cheer. Loftus concluded his speech with a stern warning that any further pro-German activity at the Herrick mines would be met with swift action by the government. The fifteen prisoners were loaded into the automobiles amid continued cheers from the other miners, and were driven out of Steubenville to the county jail to face arraignment. Later ten of the men were released on parole and compelled to make weekly reports of their conduct. At the first sign of disloyalty they were to be rearrested and interned. The other Austrian miners that had been seized were held until after the armistice.

Four months after the Praeger hanging, President Wilson took a public stance against mob violence. In a speech delivered on July 26, 1918, he declared that "mob violence is a betrayal of democracy; lynchers are no better than Germany's army outlaws. Every lynching is a blow at the heart of ordered law and human justice. No man who loves America, no man who really cares for her fame and honor and character, or who is truly loyal to her institutions can justify mob action . . . I, therefore, very earnestly and solemnly beg that the Governors of all the States, the law officers of every community, and above all, the men and women of every community in the United States, all who revere America and wish to keep her name without stain or reproach, will cooperate not passively merely, but actively and watchfully—to make an end of this disgraceful evil."

The American Protective League National Headquarters published the text of Wilson's speech in the August 10, 1918, edition of the League's *The Spy Glass* newsletter. In the same article, members were cautioned against taking part in mob activities and told to ensure that innocent alien enemies were protected from injustice:

> League members are, in a special sense, guardians of the country's internal frontier against such outbreaks as the President deplores. Concentration on alien enemy activities, on pro-German propaganda and anti-American sabotage, should not close the eyes of local Chiefs and individual members to the possibility that injustice and personal injury may thus be done to alien enemies quite innocent of wrong doing . . . The good name of the League is sometimes involved in these local "strafing" parties. For instance, Dr. H. A. Herzer, of Albion, Michigan, was recently asked to remove certain German newspapers from his waiting room table. When he refused, he was called out by a committee, stripped to the waist and given a coat of vivid green paint. In the accounts of the affair printed by the Detroit newspapers, 'the vigilance corps of the American Protective League' was named as responsible for the outrage. This statement was untrue, of course. Retractions were made later, but like all retractions, no one of them made one-tenth the impression made by the original story. Far from bullying alien enemies, the League exists to protect them, no less than to keep them in order. The League's aim therefore—and your business—is to forestall mob action by wiping out the conditions under which loyal and peaceful citizens sometimes resort to lynch law.

As to be expected in an environment in which an individual's stature was based on his or her loyalty and harsh punishment often inflicted on the unfaithful, false allegations of disloyalty were commonplace. APL operatives were instructed that a disloyalty case could not be built on hearsay. They were to explore every avenue of investigation until the complete facts were known. In the course of these investigations it was sometimes discovered that the complaint was based entirely on spite. Personal enemies routinely sent fabricated reports of disloyalty to the Department of Justice and League division offices with the sole objective being to "get even" with the accused. In the state of Montana alone, hundreds of individuals were cleared of disloyalty allegations by APL investigations and the complainant warned "not to let it happen again." In the state of Iowa, the Davenport Division went even further, and in June 1918 eight individuals found to have filed false disloyalty complaints were summoned to the division headquarters and given the option of either paying a fine to be donated to the Red Cross or being prosecuted. All eight paid the fine.

The nationwide hunt for the "disloyal," and the punishment inflicted on those convicted of being disloyal, remained front-page news throughout 1918. Then a bigger story from Europe captured the headlines.

CHAPTER 9

THE AMERICAN PROTECTIVE
LEAGUE IS DISBANDED

Rumors of the impending armistice with Germany had been circulating through the American positions for hours. Ever since news was received of the German Kaiser's abdication the day before, anticipation had been building that a truce would soon be declared. Late on the night of Sunday, November 10, 1918, the official notification reached the various headquarters of the American army in France—an armistice would be signed at 11 a.m. the next morning. As time ticked slowly by during that long night, excitement began to grow, and doughboys began to regularly check their watches as if New Year's would be arriving early this year. At 0900 hours on November 11, American infantry northeast of Verdun began a planned advance across the muddy shell-marked landscape toward Oriens. The German defenders responded with desultory artillery and machine-gun fire. When the eleventh hour drew near, the US soldiers were halted by their officers and instructed to dig in, marking the farthest line of advance as hostilities ceased. At the appointed moment, jubilation broke across the American lines. The Americans began to yell and cheer wildly, fired celebratory shots from rifles and pistols, and threw their helmets into the air as "Old Glory" was raised on improvised flagpoles. They enjoyed a feeling of unbounded joy, believing that it was the greatest day in American history.

At long last, the war was finally over . . .

Four thousand miles away in Washington, D.C., news of the Armistice was received by the three national directors of the League with mixed emotions. Victor Elting learned that peace had been declared when he drove home to find newsboys walking the streets shouting "Extra! Extra! War is over!" Elting later reflected that at that moment he felt a great sense of relief on one hand that the killing had finally come to an end, "and on the other of regret that our work which had just then reached completion would never have a chance to fully function." Albert Briggs, who had worked longer than anyone to build the American Protective League, shared similar feelings of joy and loss. Charles Daniel Frey was relieved that he could return home to Chicago once again. Frey had wanted to resign from his position as a national director for months, since learning that his younger brother, Harry, had died in France. Harry Frey, a twenty-nine-year-old corporal with the 304th Field Artillery had been killed by a German counter-barrage in late August. With remorse over Harry's death, his advertising business in Chicago suffering from his extended absence, and under an obligation to support his late brother's family, Frey's heart was no longer in working for the League. Like thousands of other APL members around the country, Frey reflected on his departure from the League now that peace was at hand, and wondered whether the League itself would continue to exist in the future.

This had been an open question both inside and outside of the government for weeks. By the early fall of 1918, it had become clear to anyone reading the newspapers that the war in Europe would soon be over. On September 30, Bulgaria had collapsed, and a month later Turkey had signed an armistice with the Allies. On November 4, its armies crumbling, Germany's chief ally, Austria-Hungary, also accepted peace terms under a separate armistice. It was now just a matter of time before Germany capitulated as well.

The same day that Austria-Hungary exited the conflict, Chief Bielaski sent a letter to the national directors of the American Protective League to say that although some might believe that peace with Germany was at hand, "the necessity and importance for protecting from espionage the Army and property of the United States will continue for some time to come and the need for vigorous enforcement of . . . the Selective Service Act and for watchfulness for enemy propaganda and financial activity will probably increase. To achieve the greatest success, it is essential that every war activity be kept at its highest pitch at this time until the full fruits of the efforts of our armies and those of our Allies are not only in sight but actually realized." The full text of Bielaski's note was published in the League's *The Spy Glass* news bulletin, alongside an exhortation from League leadership that "for many months to come . . . the fighting front for the American Protective League is right here at home. Questions of armistice and peace terms are in the hands of (France's) Marshal Foch and President Wilson and their associates of the Allied council at Versailles. Our job is to go right on with the day's work and to see that no Hun spies or snipers mess things up in our individual sectors behind the lines."

Two weeks after the Armistice with Germany had been signed, in a letter to the national directors published in the *Washington Post* under the headline "Keep On At Work Is Plea To League," Attorney General Gregory similarly urged Briggs, Frey, and Elting to keep the officers and operatives of the League on station assisting the Department of Justice:

> The sudden termination of hostilities has reacted strongly on the public and there is everywhere evident a desire on the part of patriotic citizens heretofore intent upon winning the war to withdraw immediately from war work. Such a course if

generally followed would involve serious consequences. The American Protective League has performed a great task both in active and passive service. The number of investigations participated in by you, many of which have resulted in the uncovering of serious enemy activities and disloyalties and the apprehension and prosecution of individuals concerned, the large number of draft evaders detected and your many other activities have been an important factor in winning the war. A service of equal value has been the passive but powerful influence exerted by your organization upon alien enemies and disloyal persons. The knowledge on their part that everywhere about them were the eyes and ears of a great organization auxiliary to the government raised a fear in their hearts as to the consequences of hostile action and became a powerful deterrent of enemy and disloyal activities. These services cannot yet be dispensed with. I sincerely trust that in view of these grave considerations your members will be aroused to the need of carrying on your work for the immediate future with the fullest degree of efficiency. I earnestly ask for your continued aid and cooperation.

Gregory continued to praise the League in his annual report, released to the public on December 7. Referring to the growth of the Justice Department, which had grown to six times its size in 1916, as well as the organization of the American Protective League, he said, "It is safe to say never in its history has this country been so thoroughly policed as at the present time. When it becomes possible, through the lapse of time, to disclose fully the activities of these various secret service, their work will stand out as one of the substantial achievements of the war. They have given protection not only to the civilian population but to the armed forces, and some of their activities have also resulted in direct damage to the enemy forces abroad."

Despite the public plaudits and appeals from government officials to keep the organization intact and fully functioning, it was clear to the national directors that with the war's conclusion, the time for the American Protective League was also at an end. The wartime national emergency had been the catalyst for the creation of the League and the justification for a civilian body to be invested with investigative powers by the government. With the cessation of hostilities, they recognized that the volume of federal investigations would be reduced to a level that could be easily handled by the Department of Justice alone, and would not justify maintaining a civilian auxiliary. Briggs, Frey, and Elting were of one mind that in peacetime there was no place for organized citizen espionage, which they believed was "contrary to the spirit of democracy and dangerous in its tendencies and its results."

They were also concerned that if the League continued to exist in peacetime America, it would be directed toward combating radical movements, some of which infringed on no laws, and others that involved labor disputes. Since the members of the American Protective League were active in every trade and profession, it was inevitable that the League would be drawn into political and industrial controversies that they felt would be better handled by the Department of Justice alone. The national directors also recognized that the true strength of the League had been its ability to attract men of the highest caliber who, in the interest of winning the war, had made the work they performed for the League their top priority without regard to personal sacrifice. Now that the war had been won, the organization would lose its most capable and responsible members who would leave to resume peacetime pursuits. Last, but by no means least, the conclusion of the wartime emergency would result in contributor funding drying up. Local APL divisions would soon be deprived of the financial support required to operate.

On December 19, 1918, the national directors distributed a notice to "All Chiefs of the American Protective League" announcing that by the authority of the attorney general of the United States, the American Protective League would be formally dissolved on February 1, 1919. Each chief was instructed to carefully observe and carry out the following instructions:

1. All pending investigations must be diligently pursued and final report made prior to the date of dissolution.
2. After December 31, no new investigations or other work shall be undertaken, either by reference of the Department of Justice or from any other department or agency of the Government.
3. On the date of dissolution, all matters pending and undisposed of, with all papers, documents, and other records relating to the same, shall be turned over by each local division to the proper Department of Justice agent.
4. Upon the same date, all of the books, records, files, papers, documents, indices, enrollment cards and other papers relating to membership and organization shall be delivered by each Local Chief to such Department agent.
5. On February 1, 1919, each Local Chief shall notify all officers and members of his division of the formal dissolution of the League and of the cancellation of all credentials. From and after such date all credentials of officers and members of the League shall be void. Members, upon request, shall be permitted to retain their credentials as mementos of their service.
6. All outstanding financial obligations shall be satisfied by each local division on or before the date of dissolution. It is imperative that the League shall not be discredited by unpaid obligations.
7. Every Local Chief shall likewise inform his officers and members that the obligation to treat as absolutely confidential all information acquired by them for the Government in the service of the League will continue unbroken after the dissolution; it will . . . remain the duty of all members as loyal citizens to report all information of interest to the Government, but their authority to investigate will be at an end.

The notification closed on a congratulatory note, stating that the fine work the divisions had performed had brought expressions of gratitude from many departments of the US government. "The National Directors have reason to believe that at the time of the dissolution of the League the thanks of the government of the United States will be expressed in definite terms."

This final statement was a veiled reference to a project that Victor Elting had been working on for weeks behind closed doors in Washington—a congressional resolution extending appreciation to all members of the American Protective League for services rendered during the war. Elting had first discussed the possibility of such a resolution with Attorney General Gregory, who was supportive but dubious about the possibility of getting it through Congress. Too many congressman, he felt, would seize on the opportunity to offer thanks to other patriotic groups, complicating things to the point that the resolution would be stalled. Elting next took up the matter with Congressman Mann, who he had known for many years. Mann likewise expressed great doubt regarding the likelihood of getting it through the present session, but recommended that it be introduced by a member of the Judiciary Committee, which was in close contact with the Department of Justice. Elting took the proposal to Congressman Warren Gard of Ohio, who promptly introduced it to the House Judiciary Committee, where it was printed and released to the members for action and report. "House Joint Resolution 377 of the 65th Congress" extended the nation's gratitude to the members of the League for services rendered the government during the war "in the investigation and report of enemy activities and disloyalties in all sections; in aiding, at the request of the War Department, all local and district draft boards in the enforcement of the selective-service law and the apprehension of delinquents and deserters; in cooperating with the Military Intelligence Division of the General Staff in the gathering of information of military importance; and the investigation of the character and loyalty of applicants for Army Commissions, for passports, and for civilian service overseas; and in making investigations of various kinds for other departments, boards, and agencies of the government . . ." However, there the matter rested. The resolution died in committee before ever coming to a vote, but not before 2,000 copies were printed by the Government Printing Office and distributed to the local APL Chiefs by the National Directors as evidence of the high regard in which the League was held by Congress and its appreciation for their wartime service.

Another project underway at the National Headquarters was an official history of the American Protective League titled *The Web*, written by a bestselling author named Emerson Hough. Hough was famous for writing fictional novels about life in the Old West, with such titles as "Mississippi Bubble," "Fifty-Four-Fifty or Fight," and "The Broken Gate." He had joined the League in Chicago and then moved to Washington as a member of the Military Intelligence Division staff. After the Armistice was signed, Hough agreed to a request from the national directors to write the League's official history. Local APL division chiefs and operatives from around the country were solicited for material for the book. "Send in your most successful or baffling investigation, your best report, your most important case, the funniest episode of your career as a Government agent, the incident on which you look back with the greatest pride or satisfaction . . . If you want the work of your Division to be given proper recognition in the official story of the League's war service you must act today." The resulting work, although the best source of first-hand information on League activities during the war, is also a highly biased account, having been written primarily for an audience consisting of 250,000 APL members at a time when the amended Espionage Act was still the law of the land, and the spirit of victory was at its peak. In *The Web*, Hough chronicles the history of the League as seen through a lens that is anti-German, anti-alien, and anti-"disloyalist"—a common viewpoint in 1918 America. The terms of the contract negotiated between Frey, Hough, and the publisher, Reilly-Britton Company, included the division of a 20 percent royalty on the sale price of each book, with two-thirds going to the author and one-third to the APL's National

Headquarters. There was further agreement between the League and Reilly-Britton that the National Headquarters would receive sixteen cents for every book sold through the League's marketing efforts (such as circulating order coupons to members). With the date of dissolution fast approaching and an accumulated national headquarters debt of $9,000 in expenses to be resolved before that time, the League had a strong vested interest in *The Web* being a literary success. Since the total revenue from Hough's Western fiction exceeded $1 million, this appeared highly likely.

An additional activity aimed at eliminating the National Headquarters' outstanding debt was the sale of gold-plated badges to League members. Since agreeing to end the distribution of badges marked "Secret Service" to officers and operatives as a condition for official recognition of the League by the Justice Department in 1917, work had been underway to develop a replacement badge sanctioned by the Department. Following a protracted period spent designing the new badge, coming up with wording for the badge that was acceptable to the government, locating a vendor, and ironing out business details, a formal contract was executed with the badge manufacturer in July 1918. The new APL badge was a striking design that was marked with the member's rank, badge number, and the legend "American Protective League, Auxiliary to the US Dept. of Justice" emblazoned on an oval shield topped with a federal eagle. But further delays soon ensued. The first samples sent by the manufacturer were rejected due to poor workmanship. After that, the badge maker was unable to meet the agreed delivery deadlines. By the time the first 1918 model badges were finally received for distribution, it was late October—less than two weeks before the Armistice would be signed. In an attempt to recoup its investment in badges and help eliminate the headquarters debt, the National Directors pressed on, issuing a notice to all League divisions that orders for the new badge would be accepted until January 20, 1919. "The National Directors feel that in the years to come possession of one of these badges will be valued proof of active participation in the Great War and that members not now procuring them will be regretful when this last opportunity has passed." Like the APL members' commission cards due to expire on February 1, the Department of Justice ruled that after the war League members could retain the new badges as a memento of their wartime service.

Apart from the financial problems that the delay in introducing the badges caused the national headquarters, it also represented a missed opportunity for greater control over the League divisions as well. A strength of the American Protective League was the "top-down" approach taken in forming local divisions. Chiefs were selected from the leading businessmen in the community, who then selected the officers for their division (typically trusted business associates), who in turn chose the division's operatives. This strategy usually resulted in the formation of an able, motivated, and well-managed local organization. But the "top-down" method proved to be a double-edged sword in that the allegiance and accountability of the recruited members were to the chief and his officers, not to the League's national headquarters. Each APL division took direction regarding complaints and investigations from a special agent of the local Bureau of Investigation field office. Instead of a cohesive nationwide organization, by 1918 the League had evolved into a collection of independent local dominions—"franchises" that only looked to the "head office" for general guidance. The APL National Headquarters had limited control over activities at the local level. With so few administrators at the National Headquarters in Washington, it would have been difficult in any event to manage the 2,000 League divisions that were eventually formed. To help alleviate this situation, state inspectors were selected to supervise the activity of League divisions within each state. But in 1918, many states had no state inspector and were left to the National Headquarters staff to supervise. Those that did have a state inspector still retained a tremendous degree of autonomy, since APL National Headquarters staff and state inspectors alike had limited means to remove or discipline an incompetent or inactive chief, or return an ineffective division to efficiency. Not only did the National Directors face obstacles in exerting centralized control over the local divisions, they could not even provide the Justice Department with a master list of all League members (one of the conditions under which the organization had received official government recognition). Chiefs were loath to provide an accounting of their full membership to the National Headquarters, whether due to not wanting to reveal the true size of their division or to realizing that retaining their membership list guaranteed a strong measure of independence. As a result, the League's directors could only approximate the true size of the national organization based on the total number of member commission cards that had been printed and distributed at any point in time.

The new gold badges were seen as a means to shift the balance of power from the local APL divisions to the League's National Headquarters in Washington. The National Directors planned to make distribution of the badges contingent on receipt of special enrollment cards (one per badge) that would allow them to at last create a master file of all members of the American Protective League. The gold badges could also be used to discriminate between competent chiefs and divisions and those that were lacking, by withholding the "official APL badge" from the nonperformers. Distribution of the gold badges could be used as an occasion to call in unsatisfactory chiefs and either secure reforms or obtain their resignation. But with the delay in availability of the new gold badges until almost the date of the Armistice, this last opportunity to exercise greater control over the local divisions was lost.

After having devoted months of personal and professional time to their APL duties, with the war's conclusion the members of most divisions looked forward to being discharged from League service. But within some of the larger divisions in cities like Minneapolis, Cleveland, and Philadelphia, internal debates now raged between members who wanted their division to obey the order to disband and those who wanted to perpetuate the local organization to counter radicalism and domestic unrest in the postwar period. Bolsheviki-inspired republics were being formed in Europe as the old order disintegrated, and already Socialist agitation was on the rise in the United States. Who, it was argued, was better positioned to investigate and control this activity than the volunteer legions of the American Protective League? Despite the official instructions from Washington to cease all League activity by February 1, as the deadline approached it appeared probable that some of the more well-established divisions would continue to soldier on as independent entities in the future. Nowhere did this seem more likely than in the city of Chicago.

To quell growing dissent within the ranks in Chicago and give its members an equal voice regarding the future of the division, Chief Robert Gunn called an official meeting on the afternoon of January 25, 1919, to debate the National Directors' dissolution order. Held in the cavernous YMCA auditorium on La Salle Street, the meeting was a loud and boisterous affair, conducted like a political convention with delegates representing all departments and bureaus in attendance.

After the meeting was called to order, a resolution was introduced proposing that the Chicago Division disband as instructed. "The National Directors have decreed that on February 1, 1919 the 'League will cease to exist' . . . Therefore be it resolved that no organization of any kind or character should be created to take the place of, or perpetuate the present organization in any way or for any purpose whatsoever. . . . Any use of the name, credentials or claim of authority by or through the League will subject the individuals to severe penalties of law. . . . We [will] file with the Department of Justice and the United States Marshal a resolution that should there arise a national emergency at any time calling for the aid of such a body of men they are requested to call upon the former officers of the League for assistance, and if in the opinion of the officers the work should be undertaken they will immediately mobilize the former members of the League."

An attorney named Warren Everett rose to challenge the resolution. The Division must continue to operate, Everett argued, because organized Socialists and "Bolsheviki" presented an immediate danger to the City and to the nation. The groups that they were up against were powerful, well organized, and opposed to all forms of legitimate government. "Evil influences are at work in this country," agreed a member named Powell, "as well as all other civilized countries of the globe. The only way that we can counteract the influence and propaganda of such organizations is by a civic organization of our own formation."

But others voiced their opposition to perpetuating the Chicago Division. There was nothing that prohibited a US citizen from reporting any violation of the law to the Department of Justice, a delegate named Barnes noted, advising his fellow members, "You have no authority to investigate. Investigate means that you must go into a man's business, into his life, into his neighborhood, into his home, into every angle of this thing, and you have no authority to go into these things and you cannot as American citizens assume that authority. It was given to you by the Department of Justice. It has now been taken away."

Maintaining the Chicago Division in peacetime would result in their wartime record being tarnished by the subsequent actions of others, said a member named Hopkins. "Do we want the record we have made as members of the American Protective League brought out from time to time in an unsatisfactory light? We do not."

A delegate named Hoig asserted, "If you are going to perpetuate the League and make it effective and efficient you must have some purpose to work for. What does that purpose consist of? It consists of espionage on your neighbors. It consists of us going out to see that certain people were not elected to certain political offices. There is a purpose to which this League will finally seek its level—espionage, political purposes—that has been pointed out (by the National Directors) for the purpose of warning not only this division but every division in this country of the dangers that confront us in attempting to perpetuate this organization."

The topic of debate quickly shifted from dissolution to whether the Chicago Division records should be surrendered to the Justice Department as instructed.

Chief Gunn rose to address the assembly.

"Now I am going to speak very frankly," he said. "Labor, organized labor is running this city today and I tell you for a positive fact that the President of the Federation of Labor here can go into the Federal Building and demand any files there that he sees fit and get them, and if any of you men, or any that operate under you have run into contact with him and embarrassed him in any way and gotten him down on you, he can spread that information broadcast to be used against you. I can tell you on the authority of the ex-Division Superintendent of this city that he has been forced by his superiors to show files to that man containing the names of our operatives . . . I think you should protect the men under you and not put these names and these cases over there in the Department [of Justice]."

Several members rose in support of Chief Gunn's position, stating that if the League's records were left intact they were certain to be used for political blackmail and intimidation. A motion was introduced that all records of the Chicago Division, including the list of all members, and any investigations reports of any nature be destroyed.

As the afternoon wore on, the debate between Chicago Division members gradually dissipated. A call was made for a "rising vote" by the delegates, on the question of dissolution and on any subsequent amendments. Both the resolution to disband the Chicago Division and the motion to destroy all division files and records were carried by a majority. Within a week, the 12,000-member Chicago Division ceased to exist.

At the end of January, according to plan, the 2,000 American Protective League divisions around the country vacated their office space and dispersed. For the most part, their members agreed with the sentiment expressed in a full-page editorial placed on the cover of the final edition of *The Spy Glass* newsletter. "The League was a *wartime* agency, operating under the *war laws* of the United States depending on the *war spirit* of the people for sympathy and aid in its work, achieving its results through *wartime* patriotism. *And now the war is over.*" Though after the dissolution deadline League veterans in a few cities banded together in renamed organizations to monitor radical activities, within a short time these groups also disappeared.

Farewell gatherings, large and small, were held as the divisional offices folded. In Columbus, Ohio, 150 members of the division met to present a gold watch to their chief before departing. In Oakland, California, League members presented Crystal Simpson of the Chamber of Commerce and Mary Thomas of the local draft board with gold APL badges in recognition of the assistance provided in investigating draft evaders and "pro-Germans." In Boston, a dinner was hosted by 100 APL members and Bureau of Investigation employees in appreciation of the work of Boston BOI Superintendent G.E. Kelliher during the war. In New York City, hundreds of League members joined with A. M. Briggs, Attorney General Gregory, and BOI Chief Bielaski in attending a "Muster Out Dinner" held at the Hotel Astor, where the entertainment was provided by the Fort Slocum Artillery Band and a chorus of men singing such popular doughboy favorites as "Over There," "Pack Up All Your Troubles In Your Old Kit Bag," and "Keep the Home Fires Burning."

As a measure of appreciation to its members for their wartime service, the Chicago Division printed elaborate "Honorable Discharge" certificates that were distributed to all officers and operatives. The leadership of many local APL divisions sent letters of gratitude to their men. On February 5, 1919, Operative Bernard Lichtenstadt received such a letter from Captain Taylor of the Chicago West Division, District 15:

The record of the League will ever fill a brilliant page in American history. Its members have unselfishly performed a fine patriotic duty, frequently at great sacrifice to themselves and their families. The work of the League as a whole will no doubt be recognized, but we, your former and present Captains, who have been in constant personal contact with you during this trying period, wish to take this opportunity of expressing to you our deep appreciation of your efforts, your sacrifices, and your achievements. Your record in the district is one of which you may be justly proud. Let us hope that the friendships formed may be lasting, and that the passing years will see us as closely bound together as we are today.

An outpouring of praise for the American Protective League came from government officials representing a multitude of departments and agencies. Attorney General Gregory released the statement, "The work of your organization will long be an inspiration to all citizens to render their full measure of service to their country according to her need, without reward, and with abundant zeal." Secretary of War Baker announced, "The League has performed a service the value of which cannot be over-estimated."

In Washington, Albert Briggs and Charles Daniel Frey packed their bags and went home, while Victor Elting stayed behind to close the empty National Headquarters building and settle its final debts. Sitting in the quiet solitude of his office, he penned a poem dedicated to the members of the League:

> Silent army of three hundred thousand men
> Drawn from a thousand callings, sworn to serve, and then
> On guard throughout the land, in town and country side,
> Wherever men are working and wherever men abide.
> Unseen! No streaming pennants born by them about
> Bring praise of women and the children's shout
> No martial music when they seek their foes;
> No garb of war its just reward bestows;
> Nor does the good repute that comes to civil work
> In wartime come to them. They even seem to shirk.
> By day, by night with patience and with brain
> They serve; nor ask the people's loud acclaim
> Upon their breast their badge has inward shone
> But in the heart is pride of duty done.
> And this the glory! To have had a part
> In keeping sound and true a nation's heart.

EPILOGUE

"Service to the Government is the purpose of the League. When a member enrolls, he enlists for hard painstaking service to the Government. His reward is the knowledge that he is helping his Nation in her hour of need. The League proposes to furnish the Government a competent secret organization that will cover every source of information in our business and social life, to insure protection against our enemies."

> From the bulletin "Rules and Regulations"
> distributed by the APL New York Division
> to all members

"[The Sedition Act] serves to make enemy propaganda or native-borne sedition a hazardous undertaking in any community where League members are awake and on the job. Gone is the necessity of arguing and pleading with the pro-German, the pacifist and the native-borne disloyalist to speak with straight tongues . . . indiscriminate abuse and lying reports of what is happening here at home or overseas are going to stop. The amended law is a powerful weapon put in our hands for that very purpose. To convict a man of disloyalty or sedition you will not have to prove his hostile or disloyal intention. Like murder or burglary, espionage or sedition have become positive crimes. No one who commits them can plead innocent intent and get away with it."

> From the League's *The Spy Glass* newsletter on the passage
> of the amended Espionage Act by Congress

EPILOGUE

Whether reading a novel or watching a television show or movie, we're naturally drawn to the simplicity of a clear-cut tale of good versus evil, of right against wrong. But in real life, the distinction between hero and villain is often poorly defined, and the story of the American Protective League is no exception. During its brief twenty-two-month existence, the League was the nation's stalwart civil defense guardian, providing wartime vigilance and security; it was also an omnipresent secret police enforcing support for the war through control of public expression and actions.

The League was founded in a spirit of selfless patriotism by men of strong moral conviction and high ideals. Its officers were among the "best and the brightest" of their generation, who in turn recruited men of high caliber from within their businesses and communities to serve under them. Its members joined the organization as a means to participate in the war and in the knowledge that they would receive no monetary gain or public recognition for their service; their motivation was to have the chance to do their part to help safeguard the nation in its hour of need. Much of what the APL achieved during World War I would be considered laudable in any era. League members maintained a constant vigil at war plants to protect them against sabotage activity. They collected photographs, maps, and pictures from the public that related to enemy-occupied territory, for the use of army intelligence. During call-up periods at draft registration centers, APL members provided advice to draft registrants and assistance to draft officials. They also helped to monitor compliance with government-mandated fuel and food rationing regulations, conducted "background checks" on individuals seeking a commission in the armed forces, and participated in nightly community crime watch patrols. Many of these same tasks would later be carried out during the Second World War by other organizations.

But the American Protective League was "organized with the approval and operated under the direction of the United States Department of Justice, Bureau of Investigation," and its duties were defined in terms of supporting government laws and administration policies. During the 1917 to 1918 conflict, these laws and policies included sweeping dragnet arrests in support of the country's draft laws and "zero tolerance" for public dissent that could in any way be interpreted as counter to the US government's prosecution of the war.

The US Constitution ensures the right of citizens "to be secure in their persons, houses, papers, and effects, against unreasonable searches and seizures" and guarantees that "Congress shall make no law . . . abridging the freedom of speech, or of the press." With the "slacker raid" as the government's chief method of apprehending draft evaders and the passage by Congress of the Espionage and Sedition Act (amended Espionage Act) as a means to maintain citizen loyalty, the League was sent down a dark and twisting path. The loss of personal freedoms and liberties that the United States experienced during the war was facilitated by the very volunteer citizens vowing to protect their country. The APL rounded up and detained tens of thousands of innocent men on suspicion of draft evasion, and identified other American citizens and aliens for arrest and prosecution whose only crime was freely expressing their opinions on their government, its officials, and the war. During the "national emergency" of the First World War, the US government, the Constitution, and many of the country's leading citizens (including those of the American Protective League) became subverted by uncertainty and fear, and surrendered to the popular consensus that dissension of _any_ kind in wartime represented enemy activity. The extra-legal activities that took place during the war—search of an individual's home and arrest without warrant, dragnet-style mass roundup of suspects, and more—conditioned authorities to believe that these methods were acceptable in "time of crisis," and set the stage for similar activities to occur during the Palmer "Red raids" of 1919 and 1920.

Today, it's hard to imagine the America that existed during World War I. The immigrant groups that arrived at the turn of the twentieth century, the "hyphenated-Americans," are now an interwoven part of our national culture. Women, who could not even vote in 1918, have achieved greater equality in society and the workplace, and the segregated world of blacks in America has seen a similar transformation. In the interim, the nation has also developed a greater appreciation for the difference between legitimate dissent in time of war and treason. The United States government, comparatively modest in size during the First World War, has expanded exponentially. In 1917 the Bureau of Investigation had fewer than 400 Special Agents and only 300 support employees—a key factor in the creation of the APL. By 2011 the Federal Bureau of Investigation had 13,864 Special Agents assisted by 21,840 support staff, with a total budget of $7.9 billion and little need for the assistance of a volunteer detective force to carry out its mission.*

The American Protective League played a significant role on the American home front during World War I and then quickly receded into history. Except for an occasional mention in a book about the period or an entry in an obscure academic journal, the League and its wartime activities have largely been forgotten. But periodically during an estate sale or "spring cleaning" someone sorting through a musty attic will still pause to open an old trunk and discover a tarnished badge or a yellowed commission card and wonder, "What was the American Protective League . . . ?"

---

*According to Don Whitehead, author of *The FBI Story*, during World War II J. Edgar Hoover "turned aside a flood of offers from citizen's and civilian groups across the country who wanted to resurrect the old American Protective League of World War 1." With the powerful organization at his command, Director Hoover had no need for the aging APL veterans' services.

A BRIEF POSTSCRIPT ON THE EVENTS AND INDIVIDUALS DESCRIBED IN THIS NARRATIVE

Alexander Agassiz, the furtive German raider seized by the *USS Vicksburg* off Mazatlan, was towed to the US naval docks at San Diego after her capture. In May 1918, in a federal courtroom in Los Angeles, Maude Lochrane, the schooner's feisty owner, argued against its seizure as a prize of war. "I am pretty sure we were outside the three mile limit when we were captured and boarded," said Miss Lochrane. "If there were any arms and ammunition aboard, I didn't know of it. If any of the crew had taken an oath of allegiance to Germany, I was also in ignorance of it." Based on the evidence presented at the trial, the navy's seizure of the *Agassiz* was disallowed by the court, and the schooner was released to Miss Lochrane. In 1920, the *Alexander Agassiz* was wrecked when it ran aground at the entrance to San Francisco Bay.

Grover Cleveland Bergdoll, the "best hated man in America" and the most wanted US draft evader of the First World War, was captured on January 7, 1920, at the Bergdoll family estate by a dozen federal and Pennsylvania State law enforcement officers. Bergdoll was taken to Governor's Island in New York harbor, where he was court-martialed and sentenced to five years in prison. After serving two months of his sentence at the US Disciplinary Barracks at Fort Jay, Bergdoll requested that he be allowed to leave prison under guard in order to retrieve $150,000 in gold that he had buried in northern West Virginia to support his life on the run prior to arrest. Amazingly, the army's adjutant general approved Bergdoll's request, and he was allowed to leave prison escorted by two armed sergeants to reclaim the gold. Shortly after the treasure hunt began, however, Bergdoll's car developed engine trouble in Pennsylvania. When the party stopped at the Bergdoll family estate to repair the vehicle, Bergdoll escaped. Along with his chauffer, Grover Cleveland Bergdoll crossed into Canada, obtained a forged passport, and sailed to Eberbach, Germany, where he soon took up residence.

Despite his newfound freedom, the infamous Bergdoll remained a hunted man. In 1921, two detectives attached to the American Occupation Army, Carl Naef and Franz Zimmer, attempted to kidnap Bergdoll at gunpoint, but Bergdoll was able to knock the pistol from Naef's hand and escape at high speed in an automobile.

In 1923, a more elaborate attempt was made to abduct Bergdoll that was carried out, if not at the direction of, at least with the knowledge of, the US Army. The leader of this kidnap plot was Corliss Hooven Griffis, a reserve officer of the Army's Military Intelligence Division, who was working in France for the American Graves Registration Commission. Griffis recruited an international team to assist him in seizing Bergdoll: Karl Schmidt, a Swiss; Karl Sperber, a resident of Paris; Faust Gagarin, a Russian prince; and Eugene Nelson, an American who would act as the driver. Griffis paid each member of the team 100 to 200 francs a day, plus expenses. On the night of August 9, planning to overpower and drug the draft evader, Sperber and Schmidt hid in Bergdoll's room, while the remaining members of the kidnap team sat in a waiting car below. When Bergdoll returned to his room, the pair leapt on the unsuspecting draft evader, but Bergdoll managed to fight them off and, firing a pistol into the darkness, killed Schmidt and once again escaped capture. At their later German court trial for the kidnap attempt, Griffis, the leader of the kidnap team, stated, "Time will never eliminate the feelings of Americans in the Bergdoll case . . ."

In the ensuing years, Bergdoll married a German woman, raised a family of six children, and made a series of unsuccessful requests to receive a pardon from the United States government. In May 1939, Bergdoll departed Nazi Germany for America, saying, "I want to bring my children up in the United States." Upon his return he was once again arrested, court-martialed, and given an additional sentence of three years for his escape. Bergdoll served four years and eighteen months in military prison before being released on February 3, 1944. He returned to Pennsylvania with his family where they operated two farms. Grover Cleveland Bergdoll died of pneumonia at the age of seventy-two in January 1966.

When Bergdoll failed to appear for his draft call in August 1917, his desertion made it necessary for the Philadelphia draft board to induct the next man after Bergdoll's draft number 823 to fill the quota, as required by law. The man who served in Bergdoll's place in the US Army was Philadelphian Russell C. Gross, a manufacturing company clerk, who was killed in action on October 23, 1918, nineteen days before the armistice, while attacking a German machine gun nest in the Argonne wood with Company E, 328th Infantry. He was twenty-five years old, the same age as Bergdoll in 1918.

Albert M. Briggs continued to prosper in the advertising field after the war, becoming one of the preeminent men of his time in the field of outdoor advertising. A director of the General Outdoor Advertising Company, he also assumed a position as Vice President of a new company, Outdoor Advertising, Inc., that provided "sales assistance, advisory and research services" to advertisers, and whose operations were financed by 1,200 billboard owners throughout the country. In 1923, Briggs (along with Charles Daniel Frey and Victor Elting) received the

A BRIEF POSTSCRIPT

Médaille de la Reconnaissance Française from the French government for "particularly devoted services rendered to the French cause" in leading the American Protective League during the war. Albert Briggs died of heart disease at his estate in Long Island, New York, in March 1932 at the age of fifty-seven.

Eugene V. Debs, the Socialist politician sentenced to ten years in prison for making an antiwar speech in violation of the Espionage Act, appealed to the US Supreme Court to reverse his conviction. Debs' appeal was rejected by the court in March 1919, and the next month he reported to prison. In May 1920, Debs was nominated for the presidency at the Socialist Party convention. Convict number 9653 captured 919,302 votes in the 1920 presidential election, 3.5 percent of the popular vote in the first US election in which women were allowed to cast a ballot. During 1921, public pressure on the new Harding administration grew to pardon Debs as a prisoner of conscience. In March, Harding's attorney general, Harry Daugherty, took the unusual step of ordering the warden of the Federal Penitentiary in Atlanta to place prisoner Eugene Debs on a train to Washington, alone and unguarded, to meet with him to discuss his case. What transpired during their meeting was never revealed, but in December 1921 President Harding announced that the sentence of Debs and twenty-three other prisoners of conscience would be commuted to time served. On Christmas Day 1921, Debs walked out of the Atlanta Federal Penitentiary a free man, to the cheers and applause of all 2,300 of his fellow prisoners and a huge crowd that had assembled outside the prison, with tears running down his face. Eugene Debs' health steadily declined in the years following his incarceration, and he died of a heart attack in October 1926 at the age of seventy.

Thomas R. Gowenlock, the young adman that joined the Chicago Division in 1917 as a bureau chief while waiting to see whether America would send an army to France, and who battled radicals at the Grant Park antiwar riot, would eventually be shipped overseas with the army. Gowenlock entered the Officers Training Camp at Fort Sheridan, Illinois, in August

1917 and quickly rose through the ranks, beginning the war as a captain of infantry and finishing as Major Gowenlock, Assistant Chief of Staff, G2, First Division, AEF. Gowenlock became one of the most highly decorated Illinois veterans of the war and received the Distinguished Service Medal with a presidential citation for "meritorious and distinguished service," for leading a night patrol through "no man's land" to reconnoiter the area in front of the First Division before the St. Mihiel offensive. After the war, Gowenlock became one of the founding members of the American Legion, while his business interests transitioned from advertising to oil exploration and development. After the Japanese attack at Pearl Harbor, Illinois Governor Dwight Green named (then) Colonel Gowenlock as the special coordinator for all state and local law enforcement agencies. Thomas Gowenlock died in May 1961 at the age of seventy-four.

Franz von Rintelen, the "Dark Invader" dispatched by Germany to America to disrupt munitions shipments to the Allies, was extradited from England to the United States in 1917. Tried in federal court in New York, he was found guilty of violating federal sabotage, explosives, and state security laws and sentenced to four years in prison. As convict number 8891, von Rintelen served his sentence at the Federal Penitentiary in Atlanta at the same time as convict 9653, Eugene Debs. In von Rintelen's memoirs, he describes Debs as "a fine old fellow indeed who was rather outspoken in his political views." President Wilson pardoned von Rintelen in 1920, on the condition that he immediately leave the United States. He returned to Germany, where he resided until Hitler took power in 1933. Strongly opposed to the Nazi regime ("I hate Nazidom and all it stands for"), von Rintelen emigrated to England, where he became a close friend of Admiral Hall, the British naval officer who headed the Admiralty code-breaking section that decoded the message that had resulted in the German agent's capture in 1915. Hall located a place for von Rintelen to live, and years later, von Rintelen's daughter was a bridesmaid at the wedding of Admiral Hall's daughter. Despite his anti-Nazi viewpoint, von Rintelen was interned by the British on the Isle of Man as a potential "fifth columnist" from 1940 to 1945. Franz von Rintelen collapsed in a London subway station where he died in May 1949, at the age of seventy-two.

Bernard L. Lichtenstadt served as an operative in the Chicago Division of the American Protective League until it was disbanded in January 1919. After the war, Lichtenstadt changed his name to Bernard L. Lytton and left Chicago to begin a new life as the manager of a department store in Knoxville, Tennessee. Perhaps as the result of being called upon to collect customers' unpaid bills during the Great Depression, Lichtenstadt decided to put his APL investigatory training to work in collecting bad debts on a full-time basis and started the B.L. Lytton Collecting Agency in Knoxville. In the years following the Second World War, Lichtenstadt's health began to fail, and he died in March 1948. Shortly before his death, local businessman Nester Marx purchased the B.L. Lytton bill collection agency from him. The personal effects that Lichtenstadt had left in his office at the agency, including the items issued to him by the American Protective League, were carefully placed in boxes by Mr. Marx and stored in the attic of the Marx family home where they lay undisturbed and forgotten for sixty years until Leila and Kay discovered them in 2008.

SOURCES

Prologue

Pages 3–6. Information on the discovery of B. L. Lichtenstadt's APL items conveyed to the author by Leila Lott during a telephone interview on January 20, 2012, and in emails from Kay Edwards to the author dated August 26, 2008, and January 17, 2012.

Chapter 1: *"It Takes a Spy to Catch a Spy"*

Pages 7–8. *a pioneer in the field of outdoor advertising*: "Who's Who In Outdoor Advertising, Inc,.," *Advertising Outdoors* (July 1931): 22.

Page 8. *personally developed and handled the*: "Who's Who In Outdoor Advertising, Inc.," *Advertising Outdoors* (July 1931): 22.

Page 8. *expanding advertising business brought him great wealth*: U.S. *Census of 1930*, entry for Briggs, Albert.

Page 8. *business dealings brought him a degree of power and influence*: "Albert M. Briggs Dies: An Advertising Man," *The New York Times*, March 6, 1932, 25.

Pages 8–9. *Chairman of a committee that placed religious and uplift posters throughout the U.S.*: *Who's Who in Advertising*, (Business Service Corporation, 1916), 8.

Pages 8–9. *He was appointed a second lieutenant*: *Annual Report of the Adjutant General of the State of New York for the Year 1893*. (Albany: James B. Lyon, printer, 1894), 152.

SOURCES

Page 11. *Diplomatic relations with Germany have been severed*: Emerson Hough, *The Web* (Chicago: Reilly & Lee Company, 1919), 483.

Page 11. *I could get ten times as much done*: Hough, *Web*, 29.

Pages 11–12. *I have been thinking about your idea*: Hough, *Web*, 483.

Page 12. *I can get ten or twenty good quiet men*: Hough, *Web*, 29.

Page 12. *offered a gift of an additional fifty to seventy-five automobiles*: Hough, *Web*, 484.

Page 12. *Bielaski signaled his approval*: Hough, *Web*, 484.

Pages 12–13. *Briggs traveled to Washington*: Hough, *Web*, 484.

Pages 13–14. *Briggs set down on paper an outline*: Hough, *Web*, 484-85.

Page 14. *The organization should be handled as confidentially as practicable*: Hough, *Web*, 486.

Pages 14–15. *In the advertising man's words: very satisfactory*: Hough, *Web*, 486.

Chapter 2: Organizing the American Protective League

Pages 17–18. Information on the capture of Aguinaldo from Burke Wilkinson, *Cry Spy! True Stories of 20ᵗʰ Century Spies and Spy Catchers* (New York: Dell Publishing Company, 1969), 25-30.

Page 18. *hire of laborers in the Quartermaster's Department*: "Names of Spies on the Payroll," *The San Francisco Call*, March 25, 1901, 1.

Pages 18–19. Information on Thomas B. Crockett from *Annual Reports of the War Department for the Fiscal Year Ended June 30, 1901, Report of the Lieutenant-General Commanding the Army v.1:5* (Washington: U.S. Government Printing Office, 1901), 25, 39, 40, 98, 111.

Page 19. *from offices in the Peoples Gas Company*: Hough, *Web*, 41-42, 486.

Pages 19–20. *concentrated on cities with a large population of German aliens*: Hough, *Web*, 36.

Page 20. *Mr. Briggs is a gentleman*: Brett Page, *The Hidden Menace: Wartime Adventures of the New York Division, American Protective League* (Rochester, NY: American Protective League New York Division, Department of Rare Books and Special Collections, University of Rochester), Ch. 2, p. 3.

SOURCES

Pages 20–21. *I have been authorized by the United States Department of Justice*: Letter from Albert Briggs to F. O. Peterson, dated July 23, 1917, Frey Papers (Collection 743), Department of Special Collections, Charles E. Young Research Library, University of California, Los Angeles.

Pages 21–22. *This note will introduce you to Mr. A. M. Briggs of Chicago*: Memorandum from Bielaski to All Special Agents and Local Officers, March 22, 1917, Frey Papers (Collection 743), Department of Special Collections, Charles E. Young Research Library, University of California, Los Angeles.

Page 22. *as soon as his organization is completed*: Briggs's cover letter to Special Agents, March 27, 1917, Frey Papers (Collection 743), Department of Special Collections, Charles E. Young Research Library, University of California, Los Angeles.

Page 23. *every day saw new men enrolled*: Hough, *Web*, 181.

Page 23. Information on the size of the American Protective League, May–July 1917 from Briggs's letter to Special Agents, May 1917, Briggs letter to Chiefs, July 21, 1917, Frey Papers (Collection 743), Department of Special Collections, Charles E. Young Research Library, University of California, Los Angeles.

Pages 23–24. Background of Charles Daniel Frey from Frey letter to Louis Mack, January 10, 1918, Frey Papers (Collection 743), Department of Special Collections, Charles E. Young Research Library, University of California, Los Angeles.

Page 24. *your fame as a chap who has done things*: Briggs's letter to Frey, August 10, 1914, Frey Papers (Collection 743), Department of Special Collections, Charles E. Young Research Library, University of California, Los Angeles.

Page 24. *Frey is a genius to my mind*: Elbert Hubbard, *Hundred Point Men* (New York: W. M. Wise and Company, 1922), 380-84.

Page 24. Background of Victor Elting from Victor Elting, *Recollections of a Grandfather* (Chicago: A. Kroch, 1940), 40-67; Hough, *Web*, 33.

Pages 24–25. *only vague guidelines regarding how they were to organize their divisions*: Briggs's letter to Chiefs, March 27, 1917, and May 18, 1917, Frey Papers (Collection 743), Department of Special Collections, Charles E. Young Research Library, University of California, Los Angeles.

SOURCES

Pages 25–30. Information on Frey's organizational plan for the Chicago Division from *American Protective League Organization Book*, Headquarters Chicago Division, 1-12; *American Protective League Organization Book*, National Headquarters, 1-33, Frey Papers (Collection 743), Department of Special Collections, Charles E. Young Research Library, University of California, Los Angeles; *American Protective League Chicago District: Data Concerning Organization (Intelligence Division)*, a detailed summary of the Chicago organization prepared by the Bureau of Membership for Frey in October 1917, 1-40, Frey Papers (Collection 743), Department of Special Collections, Charles E. Young Research Library, University of California, Los Angeles.

Page 31. *Frey's Chicago Division included the following seasoned business, military, and civic leaders*: Undated, typewritten list of APL Chicago Division senior officers, Frey Papers (Collection 743), Department of Special Collections, Charles E. Young Research Library, University of California, Los Angeles.

Pages 33–34. *The Chicago Division would grow*: Hough, *Web*, 182, 184, 185.

Page 34. *Without exaggeration, I think*: Hough, *Web*, 491.

Page 34. The *New York Division had over 4,500 members*: *Hidden Menace* (manuscript), American Protective League New York Division, Department of Rare Books and Special Collections, University of Rochester, Rochester, NY, Ch. 3, p. 9.

Page 35. *The matter of government recognition is now settled*: Handwritten letter from Briggs to Frey, June 26, 1917, Frey Papers (Collection 743), Department of Special Collections, Charles E. Young Research Library, University of California, Los Angeles.

Page 36. *The chief duties of the board*: American Protective League Organization Book, National Headquarters, 11, Frey Papers (Collection 743), Department of Special Collections, Charles E. Young Research Library, University of California, Los Angeles.

Pages 36–38. Information on the Medinah Temple meeting from Hough, *Web*, 32; Charles Daniel Frey note cards for Medinah speech, Frey Papers (Collection 743), Department of Special Collections, Charles E. Young Research Library, University of California, Los Angeles.

SOURCES

Pages 38–39. *Headquarters would become a clearinghouse*: *Hidden Menace* (manuscript), American Protective League New York Division, Department of Rare Books and Special Collections, University of Rochester, Rochester, NY, Ch. 2, p. 11.

Page 39. *The League's first headquarters in Washington*: *The Spy Glass* (American Protective League newsletter; October 19, 1918): 1; *Report of C. D. Frey* (business diary), January 3, 1918, Frey Papers (Collection 743), Department of Special Collections, Charles E. Young Research Library, University of California, Los Angeles.

Page 39. *I desire to take this opportunity*: Bielaski letter to Briggs, May 3, 1917, Frey Papers (Collection 743), Department of Special Collections, Charles E. Young Research Library, University of California, Los Angeles.

Chapter 3: *Battling German Spies and Saboteurs*

Pages 41–42. Information on prewar munitions plant explosions from John Price Jones and Paul Merrick Hollister, *The German Secret Service in America* (Boston: Small, Maynard & Company, 1918), 102-04.

Page 42. *Enclosed is the circular*: Jones and Hollister, *German Secret Service*, 103.

Pages 42–43. *It is indispensable by the intermediary*: Jones and Hollister, *German Secret Service*, 102.

Pages 44–46. Information on munitions plant explosions from Jones and Hollister, *German Secret Service*, 113-114.

Page 46. *I'll buy what I can and blow up what I can't!*: Franz von Rintelen, *The Dark Invader* (New York: The Merrill Company, 1933), 74.

Page 46. *a $500,000 cable transfer had been made for him*: von Rintelen, *Dark Invader*, 75.

Pages 46–47. Information on von Rintelen's meeting with Dr. Scheele from von Rintelen, *Dark Invader*, 95-96.

Pages 47–48. Information about incendiary attacks on ships carrying Allied war cargoes from Jones and Hollister, *German Secret Service*, 159-62.

Page 48. *von Rintelen got as far as Dover*: von Rintelen, *Dark Invader*, 190-92.

Page 49. *A young German-American doctor named Anton Dilger:* Henry Landau, *The Enemy Within* (New York: G. P. Putnam's Sons), 72-73.

Pages 49–51. Information on the Black Tom explosion from "3 Dead, 12 Missing, and 30 Hurt; Loss of $40,000,000 in Explosion,", *The Syracuse Herald*, July 31, 1916, 1-2. "Munitions Explosion in New York Harbor," *The Kingston Daily Freeman*, July 31, 1916, 1.

Pages 51–52. *Much of this revenue came from the owners of large industrial concerns:* Hough, *The Web*, 32.

Page 52. *One of the largest gas mask factories: Hidden Menace* (manuscript), American Protective League New York Division, Department of Rare Books and Special Collections, University of Rochester, Rochester, NY, Ch. 2, pp. 9-10.

Page 52. *received over $400 million in contracts for war equipment:* Hough, *The Web*, 285.

Pages 52–53. *Detroit operations began in the spring of 1917:* Hough, *The Web*, 285-86.

Pages 53. *He immediately got to work reorganizing the operation:* Hough, *The Web*, 286.

Page 53. *an enormous complex of four- and six-story buildings:* Horace Lucien Arnold and Fay Leon Faurote, *Ford Methods and the Ford Shops* (New York: The Engineering Magazine Company, 1915), 25-26.

Page 53. *The War Department contracted with the Ford Motor Company:* Spencer Tucker and Priscilla Mary Roberts, *World War 1: A Student Encyclopedia* (Santa Barbara: ABC-CLIO, 2006), 690.

Page 54. *the enemy had his agents in their plants: Report of Benedict Crowell, America's Munitions 1917-1918* (Washington; Government Printing Office, 1919), 276.

Pages 54–55. Information on American Protective League operations within the Ford Motor Company from "Assail Loyalty of Henry Ford," *Indiana Evening Gazette*, July 28, 1919, 6. "Pro-Germans in Ford Plant," *The Fort Wayne News and Sentinel*, November 1, 1918, 1, 3. "Sympathizers with Germany," *The Mansfield News*, July 24, 1919, 1, 12.

Pages 55–56. *League instituted its own security system on the waterway:* Hough, *The Web*, 287-88.

SOURCES

Page 56. *suspicious activities of a man living in District 13*: Hough, *The Web*, 187-88.

Page 57. *We've got a German spy in ours*: Hough, *The Web*, 188-89.

Pages 57–59. *smaller shops were given a telephone number to call*: *Hidden Menace* (manuscript), American Protective League New York Division, Department of Rare Books and Special Collections, University of Rochester, Rochester, NY, Ch. 12, pp. 1-9.

Chapter 4: *At War with the Wobblies*

Pages 61–62. *Preamble and Constitution of the Industrial Workers of the World* (Chicago: I.W.W. Publishing Bureau, 1916), 1.

Pages 63–64. IWW tactics and methods described in Vincent St. John, *The I.W.W.: Its History, Structure, and Methods* (Chicago: I.W.W. Publishing Bureau, 1917), 1-32.

Pages 64–65. *Direct Action*: Walker C. Smith, *Sabotage: Its History, Philosophy and Function* (Chicago: I.W.W. Publishing Bureau, 1917), 1-32.

Page 65. *I am not going to justify sabotage on any moral ground*: Elizabeth Gurley Flynn, *Sabotage* (Cleveland: I.W.W. Publishing Bureau, 1916), 1-32.

Page 65. *we as members of the industrial army*: Gibbs M. Smith, *Joe Hill* (Layton, UT: Peregrine Smith Books, 1969),11.

Pages 65–66. *We will resent with all of the power at our command*: William Preston, Jr., *Aliens and Dissenters: Federal Suppression of Radicals 1903-1933* (Boston: President and Fellows of Harvard College, 1963), 88-89.

Page 66. *the convention had voted approval*: "Industrial Strike Urged," *The Daily Northwestern*, April 2, 1917, 1.

Page 67. Information on APL infiltration of the I.W.W. from Hough, *The Web*, 46.

Pages 67–68. Background information on Thomas Russell Gowenlock from Frank W. Blackmar, ed., *Kansas: A Cyclopedia of State History, Embracing Events, Institutions, Industries, Counties, Cities, Towns, Prominent Persons, etc.*, vol. III, part 2 (Chicago: Standard Publishing Co., 1912). This volume is identified at the Kansas State Historical Society as microfilm LM195. Draft Registration Card for Thomas

SOURCES

Russell Gowenlock dated June 5, 1917, Cook County, Illinois, Roll 1439758, Draft Board 13, U.S. National Archives.

Pages 68–70. Information on Gowenlock's service in the American Protective League from Thomas R. Gowenlock and Guy Murchie, Jr., *Soldiers of Darkness* (Garden City: Doubleday, Doran & Company, 1937), 39-43.

Pages 68–69. *Means was an operative of the Burns Detective Agency*: Edwin P. Hoyt, *Spectacular Rogue: Gaston B. Means* (New York: The Bobbs-Merrill Company, Inc., 1963), 35-44, 54, 57.

Pages 69–71. Information on the Grant Park Riot from "Police Club Anti-War Rioters," *Chicago Tribune,* May 28, 1917, 1, 4.

Page 70. *Three of us worked our way to the speakers' stand*: Gowenlock, *Soldiers of Darkness*, 42-43.

Pages 70–71. *An easy yell of to hell with the government*: "Police Club Anti-War Rioters," *Chicago Tribune,* May 28, 1917, 1, 4.

Page 71. *Strikes are used*: St. John, "I.W.W. Tactics or Methods," *The I.W.W.: Its History, Structure, and Methods,* 20.

Page 71. *Timber strikes against loggers and sawmills*: "Drive out 1,100 I.W.W.," *The Washington Post,* July 13, 1917, 5.

Page 71. *If necessary to support the miner's demands*: *The Washington Post,* July 13, 1917, 5.

Pages 71–72. *a request for $640 million to build an air armada*: "Air Armada Ensured," *The Washington Post,* July 14, 1917, 2.

Page 72. stories of I.W.W. chicanery and sabotage: "Deportation of Agitators Kept Up," *The Fort Wayne Journal-Gazette,* July 13, 1917, 1, 8; "Reign of Terror Has Been Inaugurated by Industrial Workers," *Hamilton Evening Journal,* 4; "Increasing Activity of I.W.W. Puts Authorities in West on Alert," *The Washington Post,* July 13, 1917, 5; "Suspect I.W.W. of Firing Large Klamath Mill," *Nevada State Journal,* July 16, 1917, 1.

Page 72. *Bielaski issued a letter to all Special Agents*: Letter from Bielaski to All Special Agents, July 17, 1917, Frey Papers (Collection 743), Department of Special Collections, Charles E. Young Research Library, University of California, Los Angeles.

Page 73. *An attached letter from the Attorney General*: Letter from Gregory to United States Attorneys, July 17, 1917, Frey Papers (Collection 743), Department of Special Collections, Charles

SOURCES

E. Young Research Library, University of California, Los Angeles.

Page 73. *Clabaugh…was placed in charge of the IWW investigation*: Hough, *The Web*, 136, 488.

Pages 73–74. *The Espionage Act had been enacted into law*: Counter-Espionage Laws of the United States (Washington, DC: American Protective League, 1918), 12-15.

Page 74. *By this time it was no longer a secret*: "United States Feeding the Exiled I.W.W.; Stern Measures with Organization Urged," *The Washington Post*, July 14, 1917, 2.

Pages 74–75. *Wobblies called for a general strike*: "Industrial Workers Threaten to Cause Industrial Trouble," *Piqua Daily Press*, August 16, 1917, 1; "Drastic Treatment for I.W.W. Threat," *The Muscatine (Iowa) Journal*, August 16, 1917, 1.

Page 76. *Three weeks later the Justice Department acted*: "Government is determined to smash treason," *The Fort Wayne Sentinel*, September 6, 1917, 1, 14; "I.W.W. Offices Raided by U.S.; Haywood Taken," *The Daily Free Press*, September 6, 1917, 1; "Nation-Wide Raid is Made on All I.W.W. Rendezvous;" *The Eau Claire Leader*, September 6, 1917, 1, 2.

Page 76. *Led to 165 I.W.W. leaders being indicted by the Chicago Grand Jury and charged with*: "Branding the I.W.W.," *The Helena Daily Independent*, September 8, 1918, 7; Hough, *The Web*, 137.

Page 76–77. *The trial of the IWW leadership*: Hough, *The Web*, 133-34,138.

Page 77. *The jury arrived at its verdict in sixty-five minutes*: "807 Years: $2,735,000 Fines for I.W.W.," *The Spy Glass*, September 7, 1918, 4.

Chapter 5: *Mounting the Slacker Raids*

Pages 79–80. Information on the Minneapolis APL Division slacker raid on the Gateway lodging house district from Anonymous ("Operative 71"), *Summary and Report of War Service* (Minneapolis: Minneapolis Division American Protective League, 1919), 5-6.

Page 81. *On the same day that Wilson signed the new draft legislation*: "Conscription Act Now Law," *The Clearfield (Pennsylvania) Progress*, May 19, 1917, 1.

Pages 81–82. *Few men would be exempt*: "Rules for the First U.S. Army Draft," *Decatur Review*, July 3, 1917, 1.

Page 82. *eighty-thousand APL members appeared at voting places*: Hough, *The Web*, 47.

Page 82. *The League would turn out again*: "Sum Up League's Service To the War Department,", *The Spy Glass* (American Protective League Newsletter), November 30, 1918, 4.

Page 83. *there was scattered opposition to the draft from the start*: "Accuse 9 of Treason," *The Washington Post*, June 5, 1917, 2.

Page 85. Information on Grover Cleveland Bergdoll from "Grover Cleveland Bergdoll Born in the United States Wanted to Fight for Germany," *Sheboygan (Wisconsin) Press*, January 8, 1920, 2; "Draft-Dodger Bergdoll Believed Still To Own Storied 'Pot of Gold'," *The Burlington (N.C.) Daily Times-News*, April 27, 1939, 2; "Draft Dodger," *Independent (Long Beach)*, February 24, 1969, 1.

Page 85. *In a general bulletin distributed*: General Bulletin from Crockett to all Chiefs, "Detection and Prosecution of Persons in Violation of Conscription Act," August 4, 1917, Frey Papers (Collection 743), Department of Special Collections, Charles E. Young Research Library, University of California, Los Angeles.

Page 85. *The Provost Marshal General and Attorney General Gregory united in a request*: Hough, *The Web*, 48.

Page 85–86. *In a letter sent to the governors of all U.S. states*: "General Crowder to Governors," *The Spy Glass*, October 19, 1918, 3.

Pages 86–87. *the Minneapolis APL Division decided to follow-up the Gateway incursion*: Anonymous, *Summary and Report of War Service*, 6.

Pages 87–88. *As a result of the activities*: Anonymous, *Summary and Report of War Service*, 3.

Page 88. Information on the slacker raids conducted during the summer of 1918 from "Combing Ohio for Slackers," *The (Massillon, Ohio) Evening Independent*, June 4, 1918, 10; "Des Moines Draft Raid," *The Waterloo (Iowa) Times-Tribune*, July 28, 1918, 11; "Slackers in Prison," *San Antonio Light*, March 22, 1918, 1; "Davenport on Slackers Trail," *The Waterloo (Iowa) Times-Tribune*, August 3, 1918, 3; "Pick Up 1,000 Suspects," *The (Logansport, Indiana) Daily Tribune*, July 10, 1918, 4; "42 Give Bonds as

Result of Saturday Raid," *The (Milwaukee) Capital Times*, July 29, 1918, 8.

Page 88. *League even joined in the hunt for Grover Cleveland Bergdoll*: "Draft Dodger Bergdoll Wanted by U.S.A.," *The Spy Glass*, July 25, 1918, 1.

Pages 89–90. Information on the Chicago slacker drive from John Bach McMaster, *History of the People of the United States: The United States in the World War* (New York: D. Appleton & Company, 1920), 45; Hough, *The Web*, 143-44.

Page 90. *reaction of Chicago's populace*: Hough, *The Web*, 145.

Page 91. *the record of desertion*: Don Whitehead, *The FBI Story* (New York: Random House, 1956), 37.

Page 91. *to take place in New York City as soon as possible*: Hough, *The Web*, 203.

Pages 91–96. Information on the New York slacker drive from Hough, *The Web*, 203-04; McMaster, *The United States in the World War*, 45-49; "Slacker Drive is Launched in New York City," *The (Xenia, Ohio) Evening Gazette*, September 3, 1918, 1; "Start Drive Today for New York Slackers," *The New York Times*, September 3, 1918, 8; "Seize 20,000 Here in Slacker Search," *The New York Times*, September 4, 1918, 1, 17; "Second Day Nets Few Slackers Here," *The New York Times*, September 5, 1918, 3; "Get 1,500 Slackers in 3-Day Roundup," *The New York Times*, September 6, 1918, 24.

Page 92. *The instructions to the members of the mixed force*: United States Department of Justice Instructions to Operatives (B), August 29, 1918, Frey Papers (Collection 743), Department of Special Collections, Charles E. Young Research Library, University of California, Los Angeles.

Pages 96–97. *An editorial published in the New York Times*: "Hunting the Slacker," *The New York Times*, September 6, 1918, 12.

Pages 97–98. *even created a furor on the floor of the United States Senate*: "Halt Senate Action upon Slacker Raids," *The New York Times*, September 7, 1918, 4.

Pages 98–100. *Gregory assumed full responsibility*: McMaster, *The United States in the World War*, 46-49.

SOURCES

Chapter 6: *Operatives and Methods*

Pages 101–103. Information on the capture of the schooner Alexander Agassiz from "Tiny German Raider Caught in Pacific," *The New York Times*, March 23, 1918, 3; "Germany Incubating Nest of Sea Vipers in Mexico," *The Fort Wayne Journal Gazette*, April 11, 1918, 6; "Germany Incubating Nest of Sea Vipers,", *The Lowell Sun* (Lowell, Massachusetts), April 9, 1918, 2.

Pages 103–104. *German plans for a reign of terror on the Pacific:* Hough, *The Web*, 352-54.

Page 104. *Every district had an APL Captain,* Strother, French, *The World's Work: A History of Our Time (Fighting Germany's Spies)* (Garden City, New York: Doubleday, Page & Company, 1918) 395.

Pages 104–105. *There were six qualities that the League sought: Hidden Menace* (manuscript), American Protective League New York Division, Department of Rare Books and Special Collections, University of Rochester, Rochester, NY, Ch. 2, p. 4.

Page 105. *Being asked to volunteer did not necessarily mean: Hidden Menace* (manuscript), American Protective League New York Division, Department of Rare Books and Special Collections, University of Rochester, Rochester, NY, Ch. 4, p. 4.

Pages 105–106. Information on APL Operative Bernard L. Lichtenstadt from *U.S. Census of 1910* Chicago entry for Lichtenstadt, Charles. "Lichtenstadt, Chas., adjuster," *1917 Chicago City Directory*, 1,079; "Charles Lichtenstadt Dies; Textile Expert and Inventor," *Chicago Daily Tribune*, March 17, 1936, 26; Bernard L. Lichtenstadt / Lillian Friedman marriage application, Cook County, February 25, 1914; "Society" (Lichtenstadt/ Friedman wedding notice), *The Fort Wayne Sentinel*, February 28, 1914, 5; "Society" (Lichtenstadt daughter birth announcement), *The Fort Wayne Sentinel*, May 21, 1915, 5; Draft Registration Card for Bernard L. Lichtenstadt dated June 5, 1917, Allen County, Ft. Wayne, Indiana, Roll 1503884, Draft Board 2, U.S. National Archives; U.S. Census of 1930 Knoxville City entry for Lytton, Bernard; "Bernard Lee Lytton" (obituary), *Knoxville News-Sentinel*, March 18, 1948, 35; "Bernard L. Lytton" (obituary), *Knoxville Journal*, March 18, 1948, 26; "B.L. Lytton Funeral Today" (obituary), *Knoxville Journal*, March 19, 1948, 30.

Pages 107–108. *took the oath of membership:* Hough, *The Web*, 37.

SOURCES

Page 108. *the expression Secret Service Agent was popularly used:* "Casting the Net for Spies in America," *The Ogden (Utah) Standard*, August 18, 1917, 25.

Page 109. Information on APL squad meetings from Anonymous, Untitled APL Chicago Division Operative Handbook, circa 1918.

Page 109–110. *Some members enjoyed a level of wealth or position:* Strother, French, *The World's Work: A History of Our Time (Fighting Germany's Spies)*, 395.

Pages 110–113, 116–119. Information on APL methods and operating procedures from Anonymous, Untitled APL Chicago Division Operative Handbook, circa 1918.

Pages 110–111. *As New York operative Brett Page observed:* Hidden Menace (manuscript), American Protective League New York Division, Department of Rare Books and Special Collections, University of Rochester, Rochester, NY, ch. 3, p. 9.

Page 112. *the enrollment of female members was officially frowned upon:* undated memorandum from the National Directors titled "Enrollment of Women,",Frey Papers (Collection 743), Department of Special Collections, Charles E. Young Research Library, University of California, Los Angeles.

Page 113. *began publication of an official newsletter:* "About the Spy Glass," *The Spy Glass*, July 12, 1918, 1; "Peace Talk and the Spy Glass," *The Spy Glass*, November 4, 1918, 4.

Page 113. *When making inquiries, operatives were taught:* "Discretion is Essential in Making Inquiries," *The Spy Glass*, August 24, 1918, 4.

Page 114. *operatives had access to the most advanced surveillance equipment:* Hough, *The Web*, 163-170.

Page 122. *The APL Operative's Handbook provided step-by-step instruction:* Hidden Menace (manuscript), American Protective League New York Division, Department of Rare Books and Special Collections, University of Rochester, Rochester, NY, ch. 6, pp. 2-3.

Page 123–126. Report on Sergeant Fred Greene by APL Operative no. 229 from Anonymous, *Summary and Report of War Service*, 18-20.

Page 127. *the potential for danger could be real:* Hough, *The Web*, 222-23.

SOURCES

Chapter 7: *In Government Service*

Pages 129–132. Information on the bombing of the Federal Building in Chicago from "Four Killed By Bomb," *The Washington Post*, September 5, 1918, 1-2; "Explode Bomb in Federal Building," *The Ogden (Utah) Examiner*, September 5, 1918, 1-2; "Inquest Begins Over Explosion Victims," *The (Cedar Rapids) Evening Gazette*, September 5, 1918, 1-2; "Holding Suspects," *The Tipton (Indiana) Daily Tribune*, September 5, 1918, 1.

Pages 132–133. *Following the explosion at the Federal Building*: Hough, *The Web*, 183; George Creel, *How We Advertised America* (New York: Harper and Brothers, 1920), 142-47.

Pages 133–134. *not the only time during the war that League members performed police patrol duties*: Anonymous, *Summary and Report of War Service*, 8-9.

Page 135. *Cleveland was in the midst of a well-publicized crime wave*: "Police, APL, United Against Crime Wave," *The Sandusky (Ohio) Register*, December 22, 1918, 1; "Saloon Robbed While Police Hunt Bandits," *The Logansport (Indiana) Daily Tribune*, December 22, 1918, 1; "APL To Fight Crime Epidemic," *The Sandusky (Ohio) Register*, December 28, 1918, 1.

Page 135–136. *League supported many other federal agencies*: Hough, *The Web*, 46-47.

Pages 136–137. *American Protective League obtain public donations*: "Report to MID on League's War Service," *The Spy Glass* (American Protective League Newsletter), December 14, 1918, 3-4; "Want Pictures of German Territory," *The Clearfield (Pennsylvania) Progress*, March 23, 1918, 1; Hough, *The Web*, 50.

Pages 137–138. *to control the country's use of fuel*: "A Big Shut Down of Nearly All Manufacturing Plants Ordered by the Government To Save Coal," *The (Riverdale, Illinois) Pointer*, January 18, 1918, 1; "This Is the Revised Fuel Order," *The Lake County Times*, January 26, 1918, 1; "Auto Owners Put on Honor in Observance of Gasless Sunday," *Janesville (Wisconsin) Daily Gazette*, August 30, 1918, 1; "Severest Cold Wave in Years," *The Fort Wayne News and Sentinel*, January 12, 1918, 1; "Observance of Lightless Nights To Be Insisted Upon," *The (Connellsville, Pennsylvania) Daily Courier*, January 4, 1918, 1; "Coal Problem Looms Large," *The Bridgeport Telegram*, September 7, 1918, 12; Anonymous,

Summary and Report of War Service, 9; Strother, French, *The World's Work: A History of Our Time (Fighting Germany's Spies)*, 58-60, 62-63; Hough, *The Web*,183.

Pages 138–139. *conserving wheat and meat products to increase the supply available*: "Food Administrator Compiles New Rulings," **Alton (Illinois) Evening Telegraph**, February 4, 1918, 1; "Dealers Notified as to Flour Purchases," **Alton (Illinois) Evening Telegraph**, February 4, 1918, 1; Strother, French, *The World's Work: A History of Our Time (Fighting Germany's Spies)*, 54-57; Hough, *The Web*,183.

Pages 139–140. *to gain custody and control of enemy property within the United States*: "To Sell Millions in Enemy Property," *The New York Times*, March 5, 1918, 1; "German Trade Grip Is Broken for Good," *The New York Times*, March 2, 1919, 1; "Kultur Outposts To Be Destroyed," *Waterloo (Iowa) Evening Courier and Reporter*, April 10 1918, 3; "Enemy Holdings in This Country Huge," *The Galveston Daily News*, April 7, 1918, 3; Strother, French, *The World's Work: A History of Our Time (Fighting Germany's Spies)*, 69; Hough, *The Web*, 95-100; "Wanted: More Millions of Enemy Property," *The Spy Glass* (American Protective League Newsletter), August 10, 1918, 3.

Pages 140–141. *upwards of 3 million investigations have been conducted*: Letter from Gregory to National Directors, November 20, 1918, Frey Papers (Collection 743), Department of Special Collections, Charles E. Young Research Library, University of California, Los Angeles.

Pages 141–146. Information on the New York gardener investigation from "Just a Poor Old Gardener," *Hidden Menace* (manuscript), American Protective League New York Division, Department of Rare Books and Special Collections, University of Rochester, Rochester, NY, ch. 11, pp. 1-12.

Pages 146–148. Information on the Krueger investigation from Hough, *The Web*, 273-74.

Pages 148–151. Information on the fraudulent draft registrant case in Minneapolis from Anonymous, *Summary and Report of War Service*, 11-12.

SOURCES

Chapter 8: *Disloyalty Is Now A Crime!*

Pages 153-155. Information on the arrest of Eugene Debs from "Socialist Chief Seized at Cleveland Rally," *The (Massillon, Ohio) Evening Independent*, July 1, 1918, 3.

Page 155. *The Chief of the APL's 261-member Canton Division*: "Credit Due Canton Men in E.V. Debs Case," *The Spy Glass* (American Protective League Newsletter), October 5, 1918, 3; U.S. Census of 1920 Canton Ohio entry for Partridge, Elton W.

Page 155. *Following Debs' arrest*: "Eugene Debs Arrested for Disloyalty," *The (Xenia, Ohio) Evening Gazette*, July 1, 1918, 1; "Socialist Chief Seized at Cleveland Rally," *The (Massillon, Ohio) Evening Independent*, July 1, 1918, 3.

Pages 155-157. *The heart of Debs' speech included*: Eugene V. Debs, "Speech of Sedition," June 23, 2010, <http://en.wikisource.org/wiki/Debs%27_Speech_of_Sedition

Page 157. *This perception was reinforced by the political dialogue*: Walter L. Haight, *Racine County in the World War: A History* (Racine, Wisconsin: Published by Walter L. Haight and Frank P. Haight, 1920), 76.

Page 158. *This viewpoint was best expressed*: "807 Years: $2,735,000 Fines for I.W.W.," *The Spy Glass*, September 7, 1918, 4.

Pages 159-160. Information on the killing of Robert Praeger from "Mob Lynches an Illinois Man After Forcing Him to Kiss the Flag," *The Racine (Wisconsin) Journal-News*, April 5, 1918, 1, 8; "Illinois Miners Hang a German," *The Fort Wayne News and Sentinel*, April 5, 1918, 1, 7; "Warning to Pro-Germans of Country," *The Warren (Pennsylvania) Evening Times*, April 5, 1918, 1, 4.

Page 161. *The lynching of Robert Praeger made newspaper headlines*: "Warning to Pro-Germans of Country," *The Warren (Pennsylvania) Evening Times*, April 5, 1918, 1.

Pages 161-162. *This view was shared by the American Protective League*: Letter from G. H. Walker (St. Louis Division Chief) to National Directors, April 3, 1918, Frey Papers (Collection 743), Department of Special Collections, Charles E. Young Research Library, University of California, Los Angeles.

Page 162. *Congress passed the Sedition Act*: "House Passes Sedition Bill," *The Indianapolis Star*, May 8, 1918, 2; "For Spy Bill Report," *The Marshfield (Wisconsin) Times*, May 8, 1918, 6.

SOURCES

Pages 162-164. *The Sedition Act became an amendment: Counter-Espionage Laws of the United States* (Washington, DC: American Protective League, 1918), 12-15, 22.

Page 164. *If you are loyal and your friends are loyal:* "The Espionage Act (editorial)," *The Logansport Pharos-Reporter*, May 8, 1918, 6.

Pages 164-165. *Under the headline 'Disloyalty Is Now A Crime':* "Disloyalty Is Now A Crime," *The Spy Glass*, June 4, 1918, 1.

Pages 165. *often conducted extensive public service advertising to enlist the aid of the public:* Hough, *The Web*, 46.

Page 165-166. *to solicit tips from the public, such as the following ad:* "Don't Criticize the Government," *Greenville (Pennsylvania) Evening Record*, May 13, 1918, 4.

Pages 166. *the medium between the public and government secret agents:* "To Aid Federal Officials," *The Piqua (Ohio) Daily Press*, December 20, 1917, 3.

Page 166-167. *In a letter sent to National Director Charles Daniel Frey:* Letter from Bishop Henderson to Frey, April 20, 1918, Frey Papers (Collection 743), Department of Special Collections, Charles E. Young Research Library, University of California, Los Angeles.

Pages 167-168. *An actual disloyalty case in St. Louis, Missouri:* Hough, *The Web*, 298-99.

Page 168. *Oakland Division dealt out its punishments:* Hough, *The Web*, 446.

Page 169. *"We had no aliens—all native born American citizens:* Hough, *The Web*, 425.

Page 169-170. *Aberdeen, South Dakota must have been a good talking point:* Hough, *The Web*, 413-15.

Page 170. *All quiet in this section:* Hough, *The Web*, 413.

Page 170. *The loyal folks were so plentiful:* Hough, *The Web*, 409.

Page 170. *A gentleman by the name of Joseph Freiheit:* Hough, *The Web*, 263.

Page 170-171. *The cashier of a bank wrote a letter:* Hough, *The Web*, 406.

Page 171. *A baker of this town named Adolph:* Hough, *The Web*, 422-23.

Page 171. *Bradford operated under cover as much as possible:* Hough, *The Web*, 372.

Page 171-172. *information on 'disloyal utterances' was provided by:* Haight, Walter L., *Racine County in the World War: A History*, 78.

SOURCES

Pages 172. *at APL headquarters from civilian Liberty Loan sellers:* "Raid on Disloyalists Made by Federal and County Authorities," *Steubenville (Ohio) Herald-Star*, September 26, 1918, 1.

Page 172-173. *pulled to a stop at the Herrick mine entrance:* "Fifteen Austrians Caught in Dragnet at Herrick Mine, Brought to Steubenville and Landed in the County Jail," *Steubenville (Ohio) Weekly Herald*, October 3, 1918, 9.

Pages 173. *the remaining miners gathered around the officers:* "Fifteen Austrians Caught in Dragnet at Herrick Mine, Brought to Steubenville and Landed in the County Jail," *Steubenville (Ohio) Weekly Herald*, October 3, 1918, 9; "Pro-German Leader and Four Other Czecho-Slovaks Arrested at Herrick Mine Held," *Steubenville (Ohio) Herald-Star*, October 4, 1918, 1.

Page 173. *Four months after the Praeger hanging:* "President Urges Stand Against Mob Law," *The Spy Glass*, August 10, 1918, 1.

Pages 175. *In the state of Montana alone:* "Citizen Sentries Walked Secret Post for Country Through the Hostilities," *The Helena Independent*, April 6, 1919, 1.

Page 175. *In the state of Iowa, the Davenport Division went even further:* "Spite Charged to 8 Persons," *The Muscatine (Iowa) Journal*, June 26, 1918, 4.

Chapter 9: *The American Protective League is Disbanded*

Page 177-178. *Rumors of the impending armistice with Germany:* "Americans Fight to Final Second," *The Bridgeport Telegram*, November 12, 1918, 2; "Americans Launched New Attack Just Before Truce Became Effective," *Logansport Pharos-Reporter*, November 12, 1918, 4; "Yankees Give Hun Parting Boot of War," *The Syracuse Herald*, November 12, 1918, 2.

Pages 178. *Victor Elting learned that peace had been declared:* Elting, *Recollections of a Grandfather*, 158.

Page 179. *the necessity and importance for protecting from espionage:* "Need of League Services Will Continue," *The Spy Glass*, November 4, 1918, 1.

Pages 179-180. *keep the officers and operatives of the League on station:* "Keep on at Work Is Plea to League," *The Washington Post*, November 22, 1918, 7.

SOURCES

Page 180. *Gregory continued to praise the League*: "Well Policed During the War; Propaganda Did Little Damage," *Brownswood Bulletin*, December 7, 1918, 5.

Pages 180-181. *it was clear to the National Directors*: Memorandum from the National Directors to All Chiefs, December 19, 1918, Frey Papers (Collection 743), Department of Special Collections, Charles E. Young Research Library, University of California, Los Angeles.

Pages 181-182. *On December 19, 1918, the National Directors distributed a notice*: Bulletin: Plan for Dissolution, National Directors to All Chiefs, Frey Papers (Collection 743), Department of Special Collections, Charles E. Young Research Library, University of California, Los Angeles.

Pages 183-184. *This final statement was a veiled reference*: Letter from Elting to Frey, December 27, 1918; Letter from Elting to Briggs, January 4, 1919, Frey Papers (Collection 743), Department of Special Collections, Charles E. Young Research Library, University of California, Los Angeles.

Page 184. *The resolution died in committee*: APL Bulletin No. 27, "Joint Resolution of Congress, Frey Papers (Collection 743), Department of Special Collections, Charles E. Young Research Library, University of California, Los Angeles.

Pages 184. *Another project now underway*: "Emerson Hough Writing League's War Story," *The Spy Glass*, December 14, 1918, 1-2.

Page 184-185. *The terms of the contract*: Letter from Frey to Elting, November 26, 1918, Frey Papers (Collection 743), Department of Special Collections, Charles E. Young Research Library, University of California, Los Angeles.

Page 185. *An additional activity aimed*: Copy of letter to the contracting manufacturer from the National Directors, October 18, 1918, Frey Papers (Collection 743), Department of Special Collections, Charles E. Young Research Library, University of California, Los Angeles.

Page 185-186. *In an attempt to recoup its investment*: Final Notice Regarding Badges from the National Directors, December 20, 1918, Frey Papers (Collection 743), Department of Special

Collections, Charles E. Young Research Library, University of California, Los Angeles.

Page 187. *The new gold badges were seen as a means*: Letter from the National Directors to the APL State Inspectors, August 26, 1918, Frey Papers (Collection 743), Department of Special Collections, Charles E. Young Research Library, University of California, Los Angeles.

Pages 187-190. Information on the Chicago Division YMCA meeting on dissolution order from "Stenographic Report of Meeting of the American Protective League Held in the YMCA Auditorium, Chicago, Illinois," January 25, 1919, Frey Papers (Collection 743), Department of Special Collections, Charles E. Young Research Library, University of California, Los Angeles.

Page 190-191. *their members agreed with the sentiment expressed*: "The League and Dissolution," *The Spy Glass*, January 25, 1919, 1.

Page 191. *In Columbus, Ohio, 150 members of the division*: "Watch Given Mr. McCune," *The Newark (Ohio) Daily Advocate*, January 22, 1919, 7.

Page 191. *In Oakland, California, League members presented*: "Women Get Honors for Help Given U.S.," *Oakland Tribune*, January 16, 1919, 9.

Page 191. *In Boston, a dinner was hosted*: "Complimentary Dinner to Superintendent G. E. Kelliher," *The Boston Globe*, January 10, 1919, 5.

Page 191. *In New York City, hundreds of League members joined*: American Protective League Muster Out Dinner (invitation), January 31, 1919, Frey Papers (Collection 743), Department of Special Collections, Charles E. Young Research Library, University of California, Los Angeles.

Page 191-192. *The record of the League will ever fill*: Letter from Taylor to Lichtenstadt, February 5, 1919, author's collection.

Pages 192. *The work of your organization will long be an inspiration*: Letter from Gregory to the National Directors, February 1, 1919, Frey Papers (Collection 743), Department of Special Collections, Charles E. Young Research Library, University of California, Los Angeles.

Page 192. *Secretary of War Baker announced*: Telegram from Baker to New York Division American Protective League, *Report of the American Protective League New York Division*, April 1919.

SOURCES

Page 192. *he penned a poem dedicated to the League*: "The League" (original poem), Frey Papers (Collection 743), Department of Special Collections, Charles E. Young Research Library, University of California, Los Angeles.

Epilogue

Page 193. *Service to the Government is the purpose of the League*: Bulletin "Rules and Regulations," American Protective League New York Division papers, University of Rochester, Rochester, NY.

Page 193. *serves to make enemy propaganda*: *The Spy Glass*, June 4, 1918, 2.

Page 196. *Director Hoover had no need for the APL member's services*: Whitehead, *The FBI Story*, 189.

Page 197. Postscript information on the Alexander Agassiz from "Fair Skipper Denies She's Adventuress," *Oakland Tribune*, April 18, 1918, 1.

Pages 197-199. Postscript information on Grover Cleveland Bergdoll from "Grover Cleveland Bergdoll Born in the United States Wanted to Fight for Germany," *Sheboygan (Wisconsin) Press*, January 8, 1920, 2; "Draft-Dodger Bergdoll Believed Still To Own Storied 'Pot of Gold,'" The *Burlington (N.C.) Daily Times-News*, April 27, 1939, 2; "Draft Dodger," *Independent (Long Beach)*, February 24, 1969, 1; Willis Thornton, "Bergdoll—The Fighting Slacker," *Olean (New York) Times Herald*, January 24, 1933, 3-4; *Escape of Grover Cleveland Bergdoll: Report of the Select Committee To Investigate Escape of General Prisoner Grover Cleveland Bergdoll*, U.S. House of Representatives, April 18, 1931, 1-6; "Griffis' Prosecutor Urges '3 Years,'" *The Hamilton (Ohio) Daily News*, December 7, 1921, 28; "50 Years Ago Today," *Delaware County (Pennsylvania) Daily Times*, September 9, 1971, 38.

Pages 199-200. Postscript information on Albert M. Briggs from "Albert M. Briggs Dies: An Advertising Man," *The New York Times*, March 6, 1932, 25.

Page 200. Postscript information on Eugene V. Debs from "Sentence of Eugene Debs Is Upheld," *Moberly (Missouri) Evening Democrat*, March 10, 1919, 1; George Rothwell Brown, "Debs Alone and Unguarded Comes to Capitol from Cell on Daugherty's Invitation," *The Washington Post*, March 25, 1921, 1; "Ovation

SOURCES

Greets Debs as Prison Doors Open for Him on Xmas Day," *The Bridgeport Telegram*, December 26, 1921, 1.

Page 200-201. Postscript information on Thomas R. Gowenlock from Gowenlock, *Soldiers of Darkness*, 44; Georg Seay Wheat, *The Story of the American Legion* (New York: G. P. Putnam's Sons, 1919), 207; "Thomas R. Gowenlock (obituary)," *Chicago Daily Tribune*, May 16, 1961, 25; "Gowenlock Funeral Will Be Tomorrow," *Chicago Daily Tribune*, May 17, 1961, 28.

Pages 201-202. Postscript information on Franz von Rintelen from von Rintelen, *Dark Invader*, 255-86; "Top Spy and Saboteur for German Kaiser Dies in London; Credited with 32 Ships," *Lubbock (Texas) Evening Journal*, May 31, 1949, 10; "German Master Spy Dies at 72," *The Billings (Montana) Gazette*, May 31, 1949, 12; "Ace Spy of Kaiser Dies a Docile Man," *The Gettysburg Times*, June 1, 1949, 2.

Pages 202. Postscript information on Bernard L. Lichtenstadt from letter from Captain Taylor to B. Lichtenstadt dated January 31, 1919, author's collection; U.S. Census of 1930 Knoxville City entry for Lytton, Bernard; "Bernard Lee Lytton" (obituary), *Knoxville News-Sentinel*, March 18, 1948, 35; "Bernard L. Lytton" (obituary), *Knoxville Journal*, March 18, 1948, 26; "B.L. Lytton Funeral Today" (obituary), *Knoxville Journal*, March 19, 1948, 30; Email from Kay Edwards to the author dated August 26, 2008.

INDEX

INDEX

INDEX

INDEX